P9-DVI-960

THE NEW ILLUSTRATED GUIDE TO

MODERN
SUB
HUNTERS

DAVID MILLER

A Salamander Book

©Salamander Books Ltd. 1992
129-137 York Way,
London N7 9LG,
United Kingdom

ISBN 0-8317-5060-X

This edition published in 1992 by
SMITHMARK Publishers, Inc.,
16 East 32nd Street, New York,
NY 10016.

SMITHMARK Books are available for
bulk purchase for sales promotion
and premium use. For details write or
telephone the Manager of Special Sales,
SMITHMARK Publishers, Inc.,
16 East 32nd Street, New York,
NY 10016. (212) 532-6660.

Credits

Author: A former serving officer in the
British Army, David Miller is now a full-
time author with a specialist knowledge
of military and technical subject matter.

Editor: Bob Munro
Line drawings: ©Greenborough
Associates, ©Siegfried Breyer,
©A.D. Baker
Picture research: Tony Moore
Filmset by The Old Mill
Color reproduction by: Scantrans Pte.
Printed in Hong Kong

Photographs: The publisher wishes to
thank all the official international,
governmental archives, weapons
systems manufacturers and private
collections who have supplied
photographs for this book.

Contents

Vessels and aircraft are arranged alphabetically by nation of origin under separate headings according to weapon type.

Introduction

Today the oceans of the world are militarily important as never before, due principally, but by no means entirely, to the Fleet Ballistic Missile Submarine (SSBN). Furthermore, submarine detection is still a very imprecise science, and so the SSBN is currently the ultimate deterrent since it provides a survivable, counter-value weapon system. Additional urgency is being lent to the anti-submarine battle by the probability that submarine-launched ballistic missiles (SLBM) may soon be fitted with manoeuvrable re-entry vehicles (MaRV), which, because they have on-board navigation facilities, will have an accuracy measurable in tens of metres, thus gaining a first-strike, counter-force role. In addition to this, however, the development of submarine-launched cruise missiles (SLCM) with nuclear warheads and a land-attack role is a threat which must be taken very seriously as was shown by US Navy submarine-launched Tomahawk missiles in the 1991 Gulf War.

Nuclear-powered attack submarines (SSN) have introduced a major threat both to hostile submarines and to surface shipping, because they can travel great distances at great speed; not only are they more difficult to find, but they are also much more difficult to attack with any reasonable hope of success. The latest Russian SSN, for example, is actually faster than any torpedo that can be sent against it, introducing a totally new element to the anti-submarine warfare (ASW) problems facing a fleet commander. The nature of the SSN threat was shown very clearly during the South Atlantic War of 1982, when the presence of five Royal Navy SSNs (coupled with the sinking of the cruiser *General Belgrano*, which showed the intention to

Below: The massive form of a US Navy class SSBN (note the 24 missile silos), flanked by a pair of the considerably smaller Los Angeles class hunter-killer boats. These designs represent the two basic types of nuclear-powered submarine in service today.

use them) kept the Argentine fleet within the 12-mile (19.3km) limit throughout the most critical period of the war. If the nuclear-powered boats have tended to capture the popular attention, the continued importance of conventional diesel-electric submarines (SSK) should not be underestimated. Not only are these the one type of submarine that most navies can afford, but they also have certain capabilities which the nuclear boats still cannot match.

To counter these threats from below the surface of the oceans the world's navies are spending increasing amounts of money on ASW, resources being allocated in five main areas. The first is surveillance, which covers everything from spies reporting that submarines have left port to complete satellites and vast networks of monitoring devices permanently positioned on the ocean beds. Second come sub

marines themselves, which in many circumstances are the best ASW systems of all. Third is land-based aircraft, which are becoming more sophisticated and expensive, as is the fourth element, ship-based aircraft, both fixed- and rotary-wing. Finally, the multiplicity of sensors and the vast number of platforms combine to produce information in such enormous quantities that the whole question of data handling is becoming ever more pressing.

During the Cold War the maritime problems facing the two superpowers and their allies were quite dissimilar, because geography served the two sides in different ways. The West needed ASW for two major tasks: to protect surface ships and to detect SSBNs. The Soviet Navy, however, did not need to protect essential convoys, and its surface task groups were, in the final analysis, expendable; thus

Below: A normal day's deployment of SSBNs — prior to the ending of the Cold War and the dissolution of the Soviet Union. Most of the boats are located 'on station', a few are in stransit. Such deployments still act as a guarantee of peace.

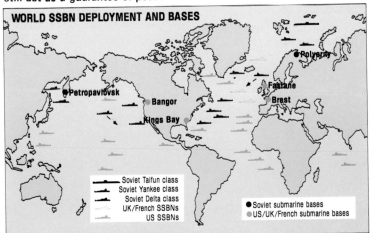

WORLD SSBN DEPLOYMENT AND BASES

Polyarny

Petropavlovsk

Faslane

Bangor

Brest

Kings Bay

Soviet Taifun class
Soviet Yankee class
Soviet Delta class
UK/French SSBNs
US SSBNs

● Soviet submarine bases
○ US/UK/French submarine bases

THE WORLD'S NUCLEAR/CRUISE MISSILE SUBMARINES

Country	SSBNs		SSNs			SSGN/SSGs*		
	In service	On order	In service	In reserve	On order	In service	In service	On order
China (PRC)	1	1 + ?	4	—	?	—	—	—
France	6	2	5	—	3	—	—	—
CIS**	63	?	80	?	?	65	—	?
UK	4	4	16	—	—	—	—	—
USA	27	7	93	—	22	—	—	—

*The USSR was the only country to deploy submarines specially equipped to fire cruise missiles. New types of cruise missile launched from torpedo tubes, developed in the USA and USSR, make a specialised submarine design irrelevant. Figures for CIS** are approximate.

their only critical role was to protect their own SSBNs. To attack NATO SSBNs or surface task groups or convoys, CIS ASW forces must pass through chokepoints dominated by NATO, e.g. the GIUK (Greenland-Iceland-UK) Gap.

Until recently ASW was a tactical pursuit, since the only threat came from torpedoes. In World War II torpedo range was at best some 11,000yd (10km), and this determined the range at which detection was necessary. Today, however, three major changes have occurred. First, the range of torpedoes has greatly increased — the US Mk 48 torpedo, for ex-ample, has a range of some 30 miles (48km). Second, an increasing number of boats are being fitted with submarine-launched cruise missiles (SLCM): the earliest of these had an anti-ship role, but new types now entering service have nuclear warheads to attack land targets and the latest, the SS-N-21, has a.range of 1,864 miles (3,000km). Third, the SLBMs now have such great range that their launch vessels, the SSBNs, do not even need to leave their own territorial waters to launch a missile against the enemy homeland. Thus whereas in World War II the ASW sphere of involvement was

Below: One of the US Navy's submarine-launched cruise missiles breaks the surface after an underwater launch. Missiles such as these are launched from the torpedo tubes or via vertical tubes mounted in a submarine's upper casing.

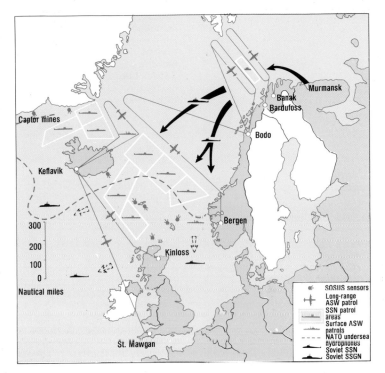

Above: This map, adapted from a CIS source, illustrates how the co-ordinated NATO ASW force is deployed in and around the GIUK Gap to intercept elements of the CIS Navy's Northern Fleet.

a circle some 20 miles (32km) in radius around a surface task group or a convoy, the area now to be covered is the entire ocean.

Many centuries of seafaring have given the impression that Man was starting to understand the oceans, but it is only now being realised that this knowledge is, both literally and metaphorically, confined to the surface and that there is actually an enormous three-dimensional world about which little is known. Indeed, more is probably known about the topography, climate, environment and resources of the Moon than about the oceans of planet Earth.

Nuclear-Powered Ballistic Missile Submarines

By far the most important underwater weapons systems are nuclear-powered ballistic missile submarines, and these are the targets of most ASW activity. It

is, therefore, worth having a closer look at them and their characteristics.

Most SSBNs carry 16 SLBMs, although some of the older CIS Navy types carry 12, while the latest CIS Navy Taifun class (DoD: Typhoon) carries 20 and the US Ohio class 24. SSBNs move fast out to their patrol areas and then cruise at about 3kt, varying their depth to make maximum use of the changing properties of the oceans and thus avoid detection. Most SSBNs launch their missiles from a depth of some 300ft (91m) in a 'ripple' spread over some 12-15 minutes, although the Taifun class has been observed firing a number of missiles simultaneously. SLBM accuracy is currently much less than that for land-based ICBMs, due to the difficulty of establishing the *precise* location of the launching submarine; SLBMs are, therefore,

Left: A Trident C-4 SLBM is launched from a submerged Ohio class SSBN. The Cold War may be over, but both the USA and the CIS still possess enough SSBNs to guarantee the destruction of the other many times over.

Right: All navies are making efforts to improve abilities to detect underwater targets. One of the most effective of today's sensors, as used by surface ships, is the Variable Depth Sonar which is streamed from the stern. Submarines are equipped with similar devices.

used against area targets (cities, industry, airfields). SSBNs are virtually untrackable in the current state of the ASW art, and thus provide both sides with a guaranteed retaliatory capability.

The main part of the US Navy's SSBN fleet is the 31 boats of the Lafayette/Franklin class, constructed 1961-66. They were all converted to take the Poseidon C-3 SLBM between 1969 and 1978, and 12 of these boats have been further converted to take the Trident I C-4 missile. The Ohio class are designed specifically for the Trident missile — 13 are now in service, with another seven building. They carry 24 SLBMs, and the hull design is much quieter than previous SSBNs, making acoustic detection by hostile ASW forces much more difficult. The big increase in range of the Trident enables these boats to aim their missiles at any target in the world whilst remaining in US-dominated waters.

Good management has enabled the US Navy always to keep about 55 per cent of its SSBN force at sea, and this will increase to 65-70 per cent with the Ohios. The SSBN force gives the USA the assurance of a second-strike retaliatory capability, but there is concern about the survivability of the communications system, although a high degree of redundancy gives a reasonable pro-

spect of getting the critical messages through. Navigation and position-fixing problems are slowly being mastered; indeed, US SLBMs have now gained a first-strike capability.

The CIS Navy's Yankee class SSBN appeared in 1968, a total of 34 being built. Due to the relatively short range of the SS-N-6 missile, Yankee-Is deploy close to the US coast to obtain adequate coverage of target areas such as SAC bases, a coincidental advantage being that the resulting 6- to 10-minute depressed-trajectory flight would prevent counter-surprise scrambles at the target airfields. Yankee-Is are being progressively converted to the attack (SSN) role to keep within the SALT-II limits as new Delta IVs join the CIS Navy. Fourteen Yankee-Is remain, together with the sole Yankee-II fitted with SS-N-17 missiles. Eighteen Delta-I SSBNs each carry 12 SS-N-8 SLBMs; these were replaced in production by the Delta-II with 16 SS-N-8s, but only four were built as the Delta-III (14 in service) then appeared with 16 SS-N-18 missiles, the first Soviet SLBMs with multiple independent re-entry vehicle (MIRV) warheads. The first Taifun class SSBN was launched in 1980 and a further five were built. These monsters (25,000 tons submerged) each carry 20 SS-N-20s forward of the sail in a unique arrangement, and

all are now operational. Despite having so many SSBNs in service, the Soviet Navy maintained only about 13 on patrol and today's CIS Navy even fewer.

Only three other navies possess SSBNs. The French Navy currently has six SSBNs, five with M4 missiles and one with the older M20. An entirely new class of SSBNs will come into service in the late 1990s. The Royal Navy possesses four SSBNs with Polaris A-3 SLBMs, but these have been upgraded with advanced warheads under the Chevaline programme. Four new Vanguard class submarines will come into service in the 1990s armed with the Trident II D-5 missile. The Royal Navy guarantees to have one SSBN on patrol at any one time, but with a second frequently also at sea. The fifth navy with SSBNs is that of the People's Republic of China. The first sea launch of a Chinese SLBM took place on 10 October 1982 (CSS-NX-3), and the missile is currently being deployed in the Xia class SSBN.

In a period of tension, all navies would obviously attempt to deploy more of their submarines — which is why knowledge of what the other side is maintaining on station is at all times of vital importance.

Noise

A submarine moving in the ocean has a number of characteristics and produces a number of effects, some or all of

Below: The colossal size of the Taifun (Typhoon) class SSBN can be appreciated in this view. Twenty SS-N-20 SLBMs are carried, each with six to nine 100kT MIRV warheads.

which may be utilised to detect its presence. Efforts are being made all the time to refine existing methods and to discover new ones in order to make the detection and localisation of a hostile submarine quicker, more accurate and less prone to the vagaries of transitory and often capricious oceanic conditions.

The first characteristic of a submerged submarine is that it creates hydrodynamic noise, resulting from the flow of water over the hull and accentuated by protrusions or orifices such as bollards or free-flood holes. Such noise can be reduced by retractable domes, bollards, etc., and by remotely activated doors over periscopes and antennas on top of the fin. Another factor in the noise problem is that long towing wires for antennas or variable-depth sonars (VDS) may themselves vibrate at their natural frequency.

Nuclear-powered submarines have a particular difficulty with respect to machinery noise, owing to unbalanced rotating parts (turbine blades, gears and pumps) and the cavitation noise of fluids travelling round a closed-loop internal system under pressure. The US Navy has gone to great lengths to reduce the internal noise of its SSNs: turbo-electric drive has been tried, thus dispensing with the need for steam turbines and noisy gear trains; and the S5G natural circulation reactor has been tested, doing away with reactor coolant pumps and the associated electrical and control equipment. These remain, however, one-off experiments.

Most submarines have only one propeller, although CIS Navy SSBNs and older SSNs have two.

Propeller noise is generated mainly by tip-vortex cavitation, in which air-bubbles at the blade tips collapse with a hissing sound, radiating mostly in a horizontal plane in line with the blades. The noise increases with the momentum of the blades and is most pronounced at high speed, during acceleration and during manoeuvres. At lower speeds such propeller noise is modulated at the natural frequency of the blades themselves to produce a characteristic 'beat', which is used for the identification of individual submarines. The use of two propellers accentuates these effects.

Magnetic Effects

A submarine hull is a large metal body which, when it moves, is cutting through the lines of force of the Earth's magnetic field. This creates a 'magnetic anomaly' which is detectable, especially by an airborne sensor. All advanced ASW aircraft are fitted with a Magnetic Anomaly Detector (MAD), which is not suitable for area search but is invaluable in locating precisely a target detected by other means. Submarines can also be detected by the electrical and magnetic fields they themselves create. There are electro-chemical processes on the hull of a submarine which generate varying electrical potentials, and an electric current flows between them, using sea water as the conductor. The rate of change of the electrical and electro-magnetic fields can be discerned by very sensitive detectors such as large electric coils placed on the sea bed.

A submerged submarine leaves a wake, which can be detected by active sonar. Further,

Left: A Lockheed S-3 Viking with its Magnetic Anomaly Detection (MAD) 'sting' extended to its full length. A MAD unit is found on virtually all ASW aircraft.

Above: Presenting only a limited visual target, one of the German Navy's Type 206 SSKs runs just below the surface. Conventional submarines must on occasion come up to 'breathe'.

the turbulence eventually reaches the surface, where it causes tiny variations in the wave pattern which are detectable by Over-The-Horizon Backscatter (OTH-B) radar. The wake turbulence also forces cold water to rise and mix with the warmer surface water, thus causing a temperature differential which can be sensed by satellite- or aircraft-mounted infra-red equipment. Moreover, when a submarine is moving at a shallow depth there is a very small but nevertheless perceptible rise in the surface of the water above the hull. This rise is potentially detectable by satellites such as the US SEASAT, which had a radio altimeter with a vertical resolution of 3.9in (10cm).

Communications

A particular problem is the need for submarines to communicate from time to time. The main means of communicating with a submerged submarine is by Very Low Frequency (VLF: 3-30KHz) radio, but external antennas are essential for reception. On patrol at its operating depth, for example, a US SSBN deploys a plastic buoy in which is embedded a crossed-loop antenna, whilst when moving at speed a wire antenna 1,673ft (510m) long must be streamed. Other com-

Below: USS *Sea Devil*, a Sturgeon class 'hunter-killer' SSN. The sail-mounted diving planes can be rotated to vertical to facilitate breaking through ice when surfacing in Arctic regions.

Left: RN sailors on a Type 22 frigate operate Type 2016 sonar displays. Sonar is by far and away the most effective sensor to be found in a surface warship's ASW inventory.

Right: The Kaman SH-2 Seasprite is one of the USN's LAMPS helicopters used for ASW work.

munications systems require a submarine to rise to some 10ft (3m) below the surface, but Extra Low Frequency (ELF: 300Hz-3KHz) transmissions can be received at depths of 328ft (100m). In addition, to update its SINS an SSBN must expose a whip antenna above the surface for some 7-13 minutes. Not surprisingly, great efforts are being made to develop some new systems of communications and navigation which would overcome such dangerous ventures to the proximity of the surface.

SSNs are faster and more agile than SSBNs, but they, too, have a need to communicate with their bases from time to time.

Below: AN/SSQ-517 sonobuoy is a passive, air-deployed sensor. Sonobuoys plan in invaluable role in ASW operations.

This was exemplified twice during the South Atlantic War. During the build-up phase in early April 1982, Nimrod aircraft based on Ascension were 'involved as communications links for the transmitting nuclear submarines' (*London Gazette*, Monday 13 December 1982), and later, on 2 May 1982, HMS *Conqueror* had to seek and then was granted authority to sink the cruiser *General Belgrano*. Any radio transmission is, of course, immediately detectable by enemy electronic surveillance, which will strive to analyse the content of the signal as well as pinpoint the site of the transmitter.

The SSK Problem

The major problem for SSKs is that they must routinely come up to the surface to obtain air to run their diesels and recharge their batteries. This can be achieved by only exposing the head of the schnorkel tube, but the latter is an easy target for modern radars and infra-red sensors. Further, the exhaust fumes from the schnorkel are detectable by 'sniffers' mounted on most ASW aircraft. Thus SSKs are faced with the contradiction that when submerged they are the quietest of all submarines and the most difficult to detect, and on the other hand are vulnerable due to this inescapable requirement to approach the surface at regular intervals.

Active Sonar

Active sonar devices transmit acoustic pulses in the audio frequency band which are reflected by a solid object such as a submarine. Pulse length and frequency are variable to suit the prevailing oceanic conditions. Range depends to a large extent upon transmission power, but the transfer of energy from the transducer to the ocean is a finite function which, if exceeded, results in cavitation and loss of power. This can only be overcome by enlarging the transmitting surface, which not only makes for complicated electronics but also can seriously affect the overall design of the ship. A further factor is that the submarine can detect an active sonar transmitter earlier than the hunter can detect the target.

Passive Detection

The main passive acoustic detector is the hydrophone, a very sensitive listening device optimised for submarine noise. Hydrophones are deployed in static arrays on the ocean bed, on buoys, on the hulls of submarines, on the keels of surface ships (although here their effectiveness is limited at speed) and in sonobouys. Both the USA and the CIS deploy arrays of hydrophones positioned on the beds of the Pacific and Atlantic Oceans, but these do little more than establish the presence of submarines and their approximate directions; a follow-up platform such as an ASW aircraft is needed for pinpointing a target. The USA is now deploying the Surveillance Towed Array Sensor System (SURTASS), in which surface ships (civilian-manned) tow detection equipment along designated patrol lines, the resulting intelligence 'take' being passed in 'real time' via satellite links to two shore-based data processing centres. Towed arrays are now also being used by both surface warships and submarines, although arrays considerably smaller than SURTASS are involved.

The amount of information concerning ocean conditions and acoustic and other detections produced by all these means is simply enormous and has led to some extremely powerful computers; in several cases, advances in computer technology have been the result purely of pressure in the ASW field. Project *Seaguard*, for example, which integrates the US ASW 'take', led to the Illiac-4 computer, which comprises 64 normal computers in parallel, sharing a 10^9-bit bulk memory. The dramatic reduction in the size of computers has led to their installation in aircraft such as the Orion, Nimrod and Viking, but most ASW helicopters still have to pass sensor data back to their parent ship.

Surface Ships

There is a long-running controversy in most navies concerning the relative merits of surface ships and submarines as ASW platforms, and there can be little doubt that there are, indeed, certain aspects of the art in which submarines are superior. Nevertheless, surface ships can also perform certain functions for which a submarine is far less effective, including, for example, giving protection to task groups centred on a carrier, or to convoys against air and surface threats. Moreover — and in certain circumstances this can be very important indeed — surface warships can give a visible indication of a "naval presence".

Although most surface warships have at least some ASW capability, specialised ASW ships fall into three main categories. At the upper end are the aircraft carriers, such as *Kiev, Moskva, Invincible, Vittorio Veneto, Giuseppe Garibaldi* and *Principe de Asturias*, which have large flight decks and aircraft which are quite specifically intended for ASW. In the middle are the cruisers, destroyers and large frigates (the categories are somewhat flexible) epitomised by *Spruance, Udaloy, Broadsword, Kortenaer* and *Georges Leygues*, which are multiple-capability ships but in which the ASW role predominates. At the lower end are the very small frigates and corvettes, such as the CIS's Pauk class, which is probably the smallest specialised ASW ship in any navy.

The ASW carriers themselves cover a broad spectrum from 15,000 tons displacement to well over 42,000 tons. Having accepted the value of the helicopter as an ASW weapons systems, these carriers represent a very effective means of providing them with an operating platform This need not be at the expense of shipborne ASW weapons and sensors, although the heavy armament of the Kiev class is only obtained at the cost of considerable ship size.

For the medium-sized ASW ships, one of the crucial design criteria is whether the ship is to have one ASW helicopter or two. Two are obviously more effective in general, but a pair are essential if the ship is to carry out solo missions. Most of this category of surface ship have, in addition to their ASW sensors and weapons, a medium-calibre gun, anti-ship missiles, short/medium-range SAMs, and CIWS. In the smaller ships a helicopter is obviously impracticable, and they tend to concentrate, therefore, upon short-range weapons (torpedo tubes and mortars) and sensors. Perhaps the finest in this category is the CIS Navy's Pauk class corvette.

One of the great problems is that all too often operational requirements staffs and designers cannot resist the desire to put more and more systems into one multi-purpose hull, which leads inexorably to larger ships, greater complexity and larger crews — and escalating costs. Unless this tendency can be resisted, many navies will find themselves able to afford fewer and fewer ships.

Right: One of the smaller-sized ASW vessels is *Abha*, an Al Madinah class frigate in service with the Royal Saudi Arabian Navy.

Niteroi Class

ASW Frigates (Brazil)

Six ships (four ASW-dedicated; two general-purpose)

Displacement: 3,200 tons standard; 3,800 tons full load.
Dimensions: Length overall 423.9ft (129.2m); beam 44.3ft (13.5m); draught 13.8ft (4.2m).
Propulsion: CODOG. 2 Rolls-Royce Olympus TM3B gas turbines, 56,000shp; 4 MTU 16V956 TB92 diesels, 19,600bhp; 2 shafts; 30.5kt.
Armament: 2 twin MM 40 Exocet SSM launchers; 2 triple SeaCat SAM launchers; 1 4.5in (114mm) DP gun; 2 Bofors 40mm, 1 Mk 15 20mm gatling CIWS; 1 Branik ASW system; 1 Bofors 375mm ASW RL; 2 triple 12.75in (324mm) Mk 32 ASW torpedo tubes; 1 depth-charge rack.
Aircraft: One Westland Lynx (SAH-11) ASW helicopter.
ASW sensors: (Hull-mounted) EDO 610E sonar; (VDS) EDO 700E.
Complement: 209.

The Brazilian Navy is the largest and most powerful in Latin America, with a manpower strength of some 35,100 officers and ratings. It operates an ASW aircraft carrier, *Minas Gerais*, six submarines and seven destroyers, together with a large number of frigates and corvettes.

In 1970 the navy was seeking new-build frigates and turned to the British firm of Vosper-Thornycroft for a basic design which could be used for both ASW and general-purpose (GP) roles. Vosper-Thornycroft had designed a very successful series of export frigates in the 1960s, and subsequently produced their Mark 10 for Brazil, of which six were built. All six have a relatively heavy weapons fit for their size. All have four Exocet SSMs, SeaCat SAMs, two Bofors 40mm AA guns, a Bofors 375mm ASW RL and six ASW torpedo tubes. The ASW version has a single Vickers 114mm DP gun on the foredeck and a Mk 20 CIWS, while the GP version has one 114mm gun (one on the foredeck and a second aft) and no Mk 20 CIWS. The ASW version is also fitted with the Branik ASW system, which is a special version of the Australian Ikara anti-submarine missile developed specifically for these ships.

Two of the four ASW frigates (*Niteroi* and *Defensora*) and both of the GP versions (*Constituiçao* and *Liberal*) were built at Woolston, near Portsmouth, while the remaining two ASW ships (*Independência* and *Uniao*) were built in Brazil, by Ast. Ilha das Cobras at Rio de Janeiro. All are due for a major modernization in the mid-1990s.

Below: Third of the Niteroi class of frigates, *Constituiçao* (F 42) was commissioned on 31 March 1978. Prominent on the foredeck is the Vickers 4.5in (114mm) gun, with the twin-tube Bofors 14.76in (375mm) trainable rocket launcher visible behind the gun turret.

Halifax Class

Helicopter-carrying frigates
One ship (FFH 330); 11 building (FFH 331-FFH 341).

Country of origin: Canada.
Displacement: 4,750 tons full load.
Dimensions: Length overall 444.6ft (135.5m); beam 53.8ft (16.4m); draught 16.1ft (4.9m).
Aircraft: One Sikorsky CH-124A Sea King ASW helicopter.
Armament: Eight Harpoon SSM launchers; two eight-cell VLS launchers for Sea Sparrow SAMs; one 2.25in (57mm) Bofors SAK Mk2 DP gun; one 0.8in (20mm) Mk 15 gatling CIWS; six 12.7in (324mm) Mk 32 ASW torpedo tubes.
Propulsion: CODOG. Two General Electric LM-2500-30 gas turbines (47,494shp); one SEMT-Pielstick 20PA6-V280-BTC diesel (11,780bhp); two shafts; 29.2kts.

Following the completion of four classes of frigate and one class of destroyers between 1951 and 1973, Canadian naval planning underwent a long period of stagnation and no further surface warships were constructed for many years. This situation was exacerbated by the abortive plans to procure no less than 12 nuclear-propelled attack submarines (SSNs): a vast programme which absorbed most of the money, resources and attention of the Royal Canadian Navy (RCN) for some years.

By the mid-1970s the RCN was faced with block obsolescence of its frigate force in the late-1980s and two steps were taken. One was the updating of the Tribal (DDH-280) class destroyers (see page 12-13) and the other the ordering

of a new design of ASW frigate — the Halifax (or "City") class. This new programme was announced in December 1977, orders being placed for six vessels
at a time. The first batch, ordered in July 1983, are being completed between
1990 and 1992, while the second batch was ordered in December 1987 for com-
missioning between 1993 and 1997. A possible third batch is still under con-
sideration, but may be replaced by an order for diesel-electric submarines. The
first-of-class, HMCS Halifax, was launched on 19 May 1988 and started her trials
on 6 August 1990.

The Halifax class ships displace 4,750 tons, large by "frigate" standards, and
are designed to accommodate a sizeable ASW helicopter, namely the CH-124A
Sea King or, in the future, the Agusta-Westland EH.101 Merlin. Main armament
comprises eight Harpoon SSMs, mounted abaft the stack, although, in order
to save money, the fire-control system for these missiles will not be of the latest
version. Air defence is provided by Sea Sparrow SAMs using eight vertical launch
tubes sited amidships, between the mast and the stack: in war an additional
twelve reloads will be carried. The gun is a 2.25in (57mm) Bofors, which although
appearing small in calibre for a warship this size, is claimed by the makers to
be more effective than any 3in (76mm) gun currently on the market (a comment
clearly aimed at the OTO Melara Compact, which is virtually the *only* 3in (76mm)
gun in production!). A US Navy developed Mk 15 0.8in (20mm) CIWS is installed,
situated aft on the hangar roof.

Considerable effort has been devoted to incorporating "stealth" features to
defeat hostile radar and sonar detection systems. There was a plan to lengthen
the hull of vessels in the second and third batches, to increase the number of
Sea Sparrows carried and to improve accommodation, but this has been shelved,

**Below: The first-of-class, HMCS *Halifax* (FFH 330), seen during its initial
sea trials. The programme has experienced several delays, but the
potential of the basic design is undoubted.**

Tribal (DDH 280) Class

Destroyers
Four ships (DDH 280 — DDH 283).

Country of origin: Canada.
Displacement: 5,100 tons full load.
Dimensions: Length overall 423ft (128.9m); beam 50ft (15.2m); draught
14.5ft (4.4m).
Aircraft: Two Sikorsky CH-124A Sea King ASW helicopters.
Armament: Mk 41 VLS for 32 Standard SM2 SAMs; one OTO Melara 3in
(76mm) DP gun; one Mk 15 0.8in (20mm) gatling CIWS; two triple Mk 32
torpedo tubes.
Propulsion: COGOG. Two GE LM-2500-30 gas turbines (47,494shp); two
GM Allison 570KF gas turbines (12,788shp); two shafts; 30kts.

For many years the Royal Canadian Navy (RCN) relied on British designs for its
destroyers and frigates, which were built in Canadian yards. In 1951, however,
they decided to build their own designs and the result has been a series of unusual
looking ships, packed with innovations and ideally suited to their role in the
inhospitable waters of the North Atlantic.

First came a series of 19 frigates, completed between 1956 and 1964. The St Laurent class (six ships) was followed by the Restigouche (three ships) and the Improved Restigouche (four ships) classes. The design was further developed into the Mackenzie class (four ships) and, finally, the Annapolis class (two ships), which is armed with two 3in (76.2mm) guns, six 12.7in (324mm) ASW torpedo tubes and one Sea King helicopter. Only the latter two classes remain in service, with the Annapolis class due to be the last to strike in 1996.

The Tribal (DDH 280) class destroyers first appeared in 1972-73. Like their predecessors they had a distinctive appearance, but this is undergoing major changes as a consequence of the 1987-1993 Tribal Update and Modernization Program (TRUMP) refits. (The specification data given above are for the post-TRUMP modified ships.) The RCN has always used larger helicopters in relation to ship size than other navies and the Tribals carry two Sea Kings. Landing is assisted by the "Beartrap", a cable which is attached to the hovering helicopter and which then hauls the aircraft onto the deck.

The new Halifax class ships (12 are on order) will join the fleet from 1992 onwards. Although designated frigates, they are actually larger than the Tribal class destroyers.

Below: A pre-TRUMP view of HMCS *Huron* (DDH 281), the second Halifax class destroyer acquired by the RCN. Note the highly distinctive angle of the funnel and the prominent 5in (127mm) foredeck gun.

Kara Class

Cruisers (CIS)
Seven ships

Displacement: 8.000 tons standard; 9,700 tons full load.
Dimensions: Length overall 568ft (173.2m); beam 59ft (18m); draught 18.7ft (5.7m).
Propulsion: COGAG: 34,000shp; 2 shafts; 34kt.
Armament: 2 quadruple SS-N-14 launchers; 2 RBU 6000 and 2 RBU 1000 launchers; 2 twin SA-N-4 launchers; 2 twin SA-N-3 launchers; 2 twin 3in (76mm) guns; 4 30mm Gatling guns; 2 quintuple 21in (533mm) torpedo tubes.
Aircraft: 1 Ka-25 Hormone-A.
ASW sensors: (Hull-mounted) MF sonar; (VDS) MF sonar.
Complement: 321.

The Kara class is a development of the Kresta-II. Gas turbine propulsion has been adopted in place of steam, leading to major changes in the layout of the midships section. Uptakes for the four large gas turbines are led up to a single, huge, square funnel, a major characteristic of the class. The Head Net-C surveillance radar antenna has been moved forward to a lattice mast on top of the large bridge to carry it clear of the hot exhausts.

Compared to the Kresta-II, a 50ft (15m) section has been added between the bridge and the tower mast to accommodate a larger calibre gun (76mm as opposed to 57mm) and the SA-N-4 close-range surface-to-air missile. Cylindrical bins for the latter are mounted on either side of the tower mast, with the adjacent Pop Group guidance radar antennas protected by high, curved blast screens. The close-in anti-missile Gatlings are abreast the funnel. One consequence of this concentration of armament in the waist of the ship is a blind arc of a full 50° aft and 20° forward for the SA-N-4 launchers, although since these missiles manoeuvre after launch this is probably not especially critical.

The ASW fit is comprehensive There are eight SS-N-14 ASW missiles in two quadruple launch bins on either side of the bridge; there are also two 12-barrel RBU 6000 launchers on the forecastle and a further two 6-barrel RBU 1000s beside the hangar aft. There is a large bow-mounted sonar and

Below: The electronics and weapons fit of a Kara class cruiser is typical of the complexity of a modern warship. Fitting all these into a hull of limited size involves many compromises, although Soviet designers seem particularly skilled in this art.

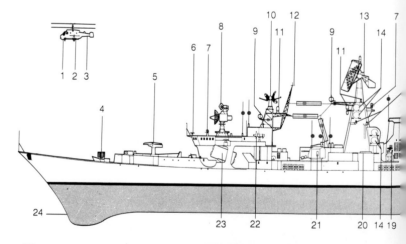

a variable-depth sonar in the stern. One Kamov Ka-25 Hormone-A ASW helicopter is carried; there is a fair-sized landing platform on the stern (above the VDS well) and a hangar with a ramp leading to the next lower deck.

The size of the bridge structure—wider, a deck higher and almost twice as long as on the *Kara*—indicates a major increase in the space available for command and control functions, but Kara deployments to date do not suggest a flagship role. Two are with the Pacific Fleet, but the remainder of the class serves in the Mediterranean and Black Seas. Production of the Karas ended in 1976, and the facilities at the Zhdanov Yard in Leningrad are now devoted to the cruiser originally designated by NATO as 'BLACKCOM 1' but now known to be the Krasina class.

Below: Kara class cruiser about to replenish from a Kazbek class fleet oiler. The landing pad and hangar for the Ka-25 are aft, and the housing for the VDS can be seen on the stern.

(1) Radar.	(7) Don Kay radar.	(13) Top Sail radar.
(2) Dunking sonar.	(8) Headlight Group B	(14) Side Globe ESM
(3) MAD.	fire control system.	antenna.
(4) Anti-submarine	(9) Cross loop HF/DF.	(15) Bass Tilt radar.
rocket launcher.	(10) Head Net C radars.	(16) Variable depth sonar.
(5) SA-N-3 launcher.	(11) Bell ECM.	(17) Torpedo tubes.
(6) Don-2 radar.	(12) High Pole IFF.	(18) Close-in weapon
		system.
		(19) Pop Group fire
		control system.
		(20) SA-N-4 launcher.
		(21) Twin 76mm gun.
		(22) Owl Screech fire
		control radar.
		(23) SS-N-14 launcher.
		(24) Hull-mounted sonar.

● HF whip aerials
● Wire antennae
(communications)

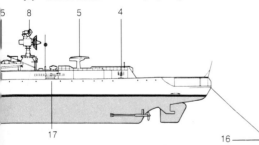

Kiev & Modified Kiev Classes

ASW aircraft carriers (CIS)
Three ships/one ship

Displacement: (**Kiev class**) 43,000 tons; (**Mod. Kiev class**) 45,000 tons.
Dimensions: Length overall 895.7ft (273m); beam 173.9ft (53m); draught (**Kiev class**) 31.2ft (9.5m); (**Mod. Kiev class**) 32.8ft (10m).
Propulsion: Geared steam turbines, 200,000shp; 4 shafts; 32kt.
Armament: (**Kiev class**) 4 twin SS-N-12 launchers; 2 twin SA-N-3B launchers; 2 twin SA-N-4 launchers (*Kiev* and *Minsk*); 4 sextuple SA-N-9 launchers (*Novorossiysk*); 1 twin SUW-N-1 launcher; 2 twin 3in (76mm) guns; 8 1.2in (30mm) guns; 2 RBU 6000 mortars; 2 quintuple 21in (533mm) torpedo tubes; (**Mod. Kiev class**) six twin SS-N-12 launchers; 4 sextuple SA-N-9 launchers; 2 3.9in (100mm) guns; 8 1.2in (30mm) guns; 2 RBU 12000 mortars.
Aircraft: 12 Yak-38 Forger-A; 1 Yak-38 Forger-B; 19 Ka-27 Helix-A; 3 Ka-25 Hormone-B.
ASW sensors: (Hull-mounted) LF sonar; (VDS) MF sonar.
Complement: 1,600.

During and after the Second World War a formidable Soviet naval air force was built up, consisting of some 4,000 fighters, bombers and reconnaissance planes. In the Khruschev reorganization this was drastically cut back and its fighters removed, but at no time was there any move back to planning aircraft carriers. In fact, arguments for and against such ships were conducted with considerable heat and vigour. The first Kresta I cruiser, commissioned in early 1967, carried a helicopter with a hangar and paved the way for the appearance a year later of *Moskva*, an 18,000-ton helicopter-carrier with eighteen Ka-25 Hormone helicopters embarked. She and her sistership *Leningrad* may well have been planned as the forerunners of a large class but no more were completed. Their duties were clearly anti-submarine as reflected in the majority of Soviet type

Below: The excellent lines and heavy armament of the Kiev class illustrate the skill and ingenuity of the CIS's naval designers. It is clear from the plan view just how the deck has been divided into flight-deck, superstructure and weapons area sections.

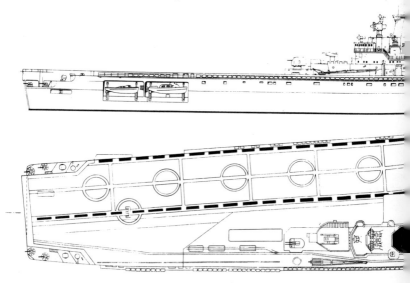

Above: Five Ka-25 Hormone-A ASW helicopters and a single Yak-38 Forger V/STOL fighter can be seen at various points on the deck of Moskva, photographed in the northern Atlantic Ocean during her first cruise outside the Black Sea. Note the angle flight deck.

designations for their major ships. They did, however, have considerable potential in other directions, such as intervention situations. Shortly before *Moskva* commissioned, the first Soviet V/STOL aircraft appeared at an air display near Moscow. Subsequently, little else was seen of this type of aircraft, but when a large hull was seen building at Nikolayov in 1971 it was no great strain on the intelligence to marry up the two.

The first British Harrier had flown in 1966 and in the next five years had carried out a series of deck-landings on the ships of several navies. When *Kiev* finally emerged from the Black Sea in August 1976 something totally new was revealed. Not only was she an aircraft carrier in all but name, she was also a very heavily-armed warship.

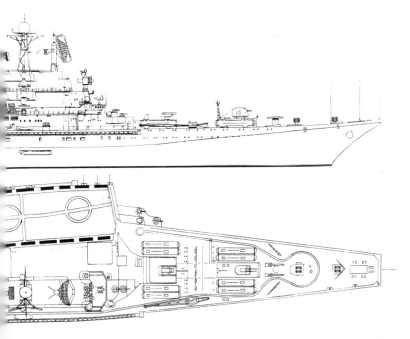

Above: A fine study of *Novorossiysk*, the third and final example of what the CIS Navy officially refers to as its takticheskoye avianosny kreyser (tactical aircraft-carrying cruiser). Clearly visible on the foredeck are the four pairs of SS-N-12 Sandbox SSM launch tubes, two pairs of which sit either side of a 3in (76mm) gun.

Right: Like *Novorossiysk, Minsk*'s foredeck is dominated by eight SS-N-12 Sandbox SSM launch tubes, for which sixteen reloads are carried. The elevated unit immediately ahead of the 3in (76mm) gun is the SUW-N-1 twin launcher, while the unit between the rear pairs of SS-N-12 tubes is a twin launcher for SA-N-3B Goblet SAMs.

Eight anti-ship missile launchers are on her foredeck, with numerous other missiles on the superstructure and 3in (76mm) guns for more conventional defence. She also carries radars and sonar — a major departure from US practice. The first-generation Yak-38 Forger aircraft took some time to work up properly but by the late-1980s were a professional force, displaying a rolling take-off capability which had hitherto been thought impossible in the West. The first two ships, *Kiev* and *Minsk*, are identical, but the third-of-class, *Novorossiysk*, introduced a number of minor changes. The fourth carrier, *Baku* (originally *Tbilisi* then *Admiral Gorshkov*) has so many changes that she is regarded as a separate class on her own. The large *Sky Watch* planar, phased-array radar mounted on the superstructure, and the *Cake Stand* cylindrical array atop before the stack are among the most obvious visual changes. There are differences in armament and various steps have been taken to improve the airflow over the flight-deck.

Krivak I-III Classes

ASW frigates (CIS)

Kirvak I — 21 ships; **Krivak II** — 11 ships; **Krivak III** — 8 ships.

Displacement: 3,170 tons standard; 3,670 full load.
Dimensions: Length overall 410.1ft (125m); beam 46.3ft (14.1m); draught 15.1ft (4.1m).
Propulsion: 4 gas turbines, 72,800shp; 2 shafts; 30kt.
Armament: 1 quadruple SS-N-14 launcher; 2 twin SA-N-4 launchers; 2 3.9in (100mm) guns; 2 RBU 6000 mortars; 2 quadruple 21in (533mm) torpedo tubes; mines.
ASW sensors: (Bow-mounted) Bull Nose MF sonar; (VDS) Mare Tail MF variable-depth sonar.
Complement: 200.
(Specification is for Krivak II class. Krivak I and III classes differ in detail.)

The Krivak class was first seen by Western observers in 1970. It was designed for, among other things, ease of construction and this has enabled it to be built by smaller yards on the Baltic and Black Seas, leaving the larger yards free to concentrate on larger and more complicated warships. To date, it has been built in three versions.

The primary mission of the Krivak Is and IIs is ASW and their primary weapon system is the SS-N-14, a torpedo-carrying missile similar in concept to the US Asroc and Australian Ikara. Four of these missiles are mounted in a large quadruple launcher on the foredeck. This is backed up by two 12-tube RBU 6000 ASW rocket launchers and by two quadruple 21in (533mm) torpedo tubes. Mine-rails are also fitted to both types. The Krivak Is have two twin 3in (76mm) gun turrets mounted aft, but in the Krivak IIs, which appeared in 1975, these have been replaced by two single 3.9in (100mm) mounts.

The first Krivak III was seen in 1984 and this version was built specifically for border patrol tasks, with the ships being operated by naval crews, but under the control of the KGB Maritime Border Guard. In this version one 3.9in (100mm) turret is installed forward, leaving the entire after end to be fitted with an ample flight-deck and hangar for a Kamov Ka-27 Helix-A ASW helicopter.

Since its first appearance the long, sleek lines and combination of powerful armament and effective propulsion system have made the Krivak class an admired sight on the world's oceans. The one disadvantage of the Krivak I and II is that they lack a helicopter facility, and although this has been resolved in the Krivak III this version is not fitted for ASW tasks. These frigates have also been used as general purpose destroyers.

Above: A Krivak II frigate in the Mediterranean. The housing and door for the VDS are prominent on the quarterdeck. Although an admired design, the lack of a helideck is a serious deficiency.

Below: The layout of the Krivak I is clearly seen in this view. ASW weapons are the foredeck SS-N-14 launchers, a pair of RBU 6000 mortars before the bridge and quad torpedo tubes amidships.

Moskva Class

ASW helicopter cruiser (CIS)
Two ships

Displacement: 19,200 tons full load.
Dimensions: Length 623.4ft (190m); beam (flightdeck) 111.9ft (34.1m), (hull) 85.3ft (26m); draught 24.9ft (7.6m).
Propulsion: Geared steam turbines, 100,000shp; 2 shafts; 30kt.
Armament: 2 twin SA-N-3 launchers; 1 twin SUW-N-1 launcher; 2 twin 2.25in (57mm) guns; 2 RBU 6000 launchers.
Aircraft: 15-18 Ka-25 Hormone-A/B/C helicopters.
ASW sensors: (Hull-mounted) LF sonar; (VDS) MF sonar.
Complement: 850.

Right: *Moskva* in the Mediterranean Sea. The heavy armament on the forecastle can be seen as can the concentration of sensors on the pyramid-shaped superstructure. The flight-deck is 265.7 x 111.9ft (81 x 34m) in size, with four helicopter spots; the Yak-36 Forger VTOL fighter cannot, however, operate from the Moskva class vessels.

Below: Two Ka-25 Hormone ASW helicopters sit with their rotor blades folded on the flight-deck of a Moskva class cruiser. The gun abreast the funnel is a twin 2.25in (57mm) dual-purpose mounting.

Above: An overhead view of *Moskva* with its two narrow lifts, which are restricted to Hormones, clearly visible on the flight-deck.

Designated 'protivolodochny kreyser' (anti-submarine cruiser) by the CIS Navy, *Moskva* first appeared in 1967 and served notice on the West that the Russians were moving into the shipborne aviation business in a big way. There is no doubt that these two well-designed ships were intended primarily to hunt US Navy SSBNs in the eastern Mediterranean, but they also served to train the former Soviet Navy ships' crews and aviators in operating large numbers of aircraft at sea. They were thus, to a large degree, stepping-stones on the way to the Kiev class.

The design of the Moskvas may have been influenced to a certain extent by the helicopter cruisers built for the French and Italian Navies in the early 1960s, but the design is much larger, able to operate an air group of fifteen-eighteen Kamov Ka-25 Hormones housed in a spacious hangar beneath the half-length flight deck. This is served by two aircraft lifts, which are somewhat narrow and limit the ship to Hormones; even the Mil Mi-8 Hip is too large to use them.

The primary ASW weapons system of the Moskvas is the Ka-25 helicopters, which are normally of the ASW Hormone-A type (qv) although some of the -B and -C versions may also be carried. Unlike Western aircraft carriers, however, the forward part of these ships is occupied by a comprehensive outfit of ASW and air defence systems. ASW sensors include a hull-mounted low-frequency sonar and a variable-depth sonar trailed from the stern. There is a twin SUW-N-1 anti-submarine missile launcher on the forecastle, and two RBU 6000 twelve-barrelled rocket launchers on the bow. There is also an SA-N-3 area air defence system, and two twin 57mm dual-purpose gun mountings seem to have been fitted almost as an afterthought. The tall, pyramid-shaped superstructure includes the bridge, the funnel and the numerous radio, radar and ESM antennas found on all Soviet warships.

Only two units of the class were built, *Moskva* and *Leningrad*, and they have served well, although CIS interest in medium-sized air-capable ships appears now to have waned in favour of the very much larger aircraft-carrying ships of the Kiev class.

Pauk Class

Fast attack craft — patrol (CIS)
Twelve ships (+)

Displacement: 700 tons full load.
Dimensions: Length overall 187ft (57m); beam 34.4ft (10.5m); draught 6.6ft (2m).
Propulsion: Diesels, 12,000shp; 2 shafts; 26kt.
Armament: 2 RBU 1200 launchers; 1 3in (76mm) gun; 1 30mm Gatling gun; 1 SA-N-5 launcher; 4 15.7in (400mm) torpedo tubes.
Aircraft: None.
ASW sensors: Dipping sonar on transom.
Complement: 80.

The Soviet Navy's Pauk design is especially interesting as being one of the smallest specialised anti-submarine ships. First seen by Western observers in 1980, Pauk is intended to be the replacement for the ageing Poti class and it would appear that, unusually for them, the Soviets have adopted the hull of the Tarantul class missile ship rather than develop a new one.

The ASW sensor and weapon fit is probably as comprehensive as could possibly be installed in a hull of this size. There is a prominent housing for a dipping sonar on the transom, making the Pauk the smallest ship to carry such a device; there may well also be a hull-mounted sonar in the bow

position, but this is as yet unconfirmed. Main ASW weapons are four single 15.7in (400mm) electric-powered acoustic homing torpedos, mounted amidships. There are also two RBU 1200 250mm ASW mortars for close-in attack and, for good measure, two six-round depth-charge racks mounted at the stern on either side of the VDS housing.

The Soviet predilection for ever larger guns is followed on the Pauk which has a single 76mm in a dual-purpose mounting on the forecastle and well clear of the superstructure, giving it an excellent field of fire. For close-in air defence there is an ADG6-30 six-barrelled 30mm Gatling on the after superstructure, together with an SA-N-5 Grail SAM launcher below it on the quarterdeck. These air defence weapons systems are controlled by a single Bass Tilt director, mounted on a pedestal at the after end of the bridge structure. The propulsion system is all-diesel, exhaust outlets being located in the hull sides. With an assessed 12,000shp, these should gvie a maximum speed in the region of 26kt.

As in so many other classes the Soviet naval architects have managed to pack a great deal into a small hull, and this class represents a substantial addition to the Soviet short-range ASW forces. Western ship designers could well take note of this class, which will undoubtedly be built in large numbers

Below: Typical of the Soviet ability to pack a lot of weapons into a small hull is this Pauk class FAC. ASW weapons include RBU 1200 launchers and torpedoes. Large stern housing is for VDS.

Udaloy Class

Destroyers (C1S)
Eleven ships

Displacement: 6,700 tons standard; 8,700 tons full load.
Dimensions: Length overall 531.4ft (162m); beam 63.3ft (19.3m); draught 20.3ft (6.2m).
Propulsion: 2 gas turbines, 30,000shp; 2 gas turbines, 6,000shp; 35kt.
Armament: 2 quadruple SS-N-14 launchers; 2 RBU 6000 launchers; 8 VLS canisters for SA-N-9; 2 3.9in (100mm) guns; 4 30mm Gatling guns; 2 quintuple 21in (533mm) torpedo tubes.
Aircraft: 2 Ka-27 Helix-A.
ASW sensors: (Hull-mounted) LF sonar; (VDS) MF sonar.
Complement: 350.

The Udaloy is of great interest because it is optimised for the ASW role and is clearly intended to be the anti-submarine component of a mixed battle group operating at some distance from its base, probably in the northern and central Atlantic. The ASW armament is exceptionally powerful. There are the now standard quadruple SS-N-14 launchers abreast the bridge, two RBU 6000 rocket launchers, and two quadruple 21in (533mm) torpedo tubes amidships. Udaloy has two separate hangars for its pair of Helix-A ASW helicopters, the first Russian cruiser or destroyer to be equipped to operate two rather than one aircraft. The landing platform is large and located above the VDS well on the stern, but the hangar floor is one deck lower with a ramp for moving the aircraft from one

level to the other. The sharp rake of the bow indicates a large low-frequency sonar dome fitted below, and this is confirmed by the characteristics of the bow wave. There is a VDS at the stern, streamed over the transom in line with Russian naval practice.

Other weapons are somewhat limited. There are two 100mm dual-purpose guns in single mountings in the 'A' and 'B' positions, together with four 30mm Gatling CIWS. Air defence is provided by eight SA-N-9 SAM launchers. Air and surface surveillance radars are also rather limited by previous standards.

In view of the similarity in dimensions and displacement between this class and the Sovremenny class, which appeared at the same time but are optimised for the anti-surface role, it is surprising that the two classes do not share a common hull. This certainly would have been the case for a Western navy, but the political and economic constraints upon the old Soviet Navy were much less severe and they were permitted to optimise the hull form as well. The propulsion method is also different, Sovremenny having steam turbines and Udaloy gas turbines (which are particularly suited for the ASW mission).

These ships are classified by the Russians as *'bol'shoy protivolodochny korabl'* (large ASW ship. BPK) and by NATO as DDGs, although their size suggests that the designation 'cruiser' is much more appropriate. Eleven vessels of this very capable and interesting class have been built.

Below: Commissioned between 1980 and 1991, the eleven Udaloy class destroyers were built as successors to the Kresta II class. Visible to the rear of this example are the two hangars, each capable of housing one Ka-27 Helix, while the foredeck is dominated by SA-N-9 launchers and the two 3.9in (100mm) guns.

Nils Juel Class

General-Purpose Frigates (Denmark)
Three ships

Displacement: 1,320 tons full load.
Dimensions: Length overall 275.6ft (84.0m); beam 33.8ft (10.3); draught 10.2ft (3.1m).
Propulsion: GODOG. 2 General Electric LM-2500 gas turbine, 28,400shp; 1 MTU 20V9S6 TB82 diesel, 4,500bhp each; 2 shafts; 30kts.
Armament: 2 quadruple Harpoon SSM launchers; 1 Mk 29 octuple, Sea Sparrow SAM launcher; 1 3in (76mm) DP gun; 4 0.8in (20mm) AA guns; 1 depth-charge rack.
ASW sensors: (hull-mounted) Plessey PMS-26 sonar.
Complement: 100.

Despite its small size the Royal Danish Navy (RDN) has a long tradition of designing and building its own warships. However, this task has been made more difficult by small budgets and the RDN has had to come up with some ingenious solutions to its problems to meet its crucial NATO mission of closing the Skagerrak to hostile forces.

For many years it operated two large Peder Skram class frigates, but these reached the end of their useful lives and were scrapped in 1991. As a result the major surface units are three Nils Juel class ships, which were built between 1976 and 1979, and which subsequently joined the RDN fleet between 1980 and 1982. They are very handsome ships, but small, displacing only 1,320 tons, and as a result have only limited sensors and weapons systems.

The main surface armament is the widely-used Harpoon missile, with two quadruple launchers abaft the stack. There is also a single 3in (76mm) OTO Melara Compact dual-purpose gun mounted on the foredeck. The Melara is capable of firing 85 rounds a minute to a range of 7 miles (12km/6.6nm) in the AA role. Other AA weapons consist of a single octuple NATO Sea Sparrow launcher aft (for which there are no reloads) and four single 20mm cannon. In an updating programme for the class, it was planned to replace the Sea Sparrows with the US Rolling Airframe Missile, with two 10-missile lightweight launchers, presumably also mounted aft, but this plan has recently been postponed indefinitely.

ASW capability is limited, the only sonar being a Plessey PMS-26. It was planned to install ASW torpedoes during construction, but this option was also cancelled and the sole ASW weapon available for use is a single depth-charge rack.

Denmark is currently building a series of Stanflex 300 multifunction ships. This is a most imaginative design in which a common hull can be adapted by use of special modules to optimise it for patrol duties, minesweeping or minelaying. Presumably, should this concept prove successful in practise, then a similar design will be developed for the ASW mission.

Below: Designed by YARD in Glasgow to RDN specifications, the Nils Juel class was commissioned in the early 1980s and at present consists of: the *Nils Juel*, *Olfert Fischer* and *Peter Tordenskiold*. The communications and combat data systems are due to undergo an update in not too distant future. This refit was also to include the introduction of two RAM launchers, but this option has now been cancelled.

Georges Leygues (F70 ASW) Class

Guided Missile Destroyers (France)
Seven ships

Displacement: 4,350 tons full load.
Dimensions: Length overall 456.0ft (139.0m); beam 45.9ft (14.0m); draught 13.5ft (4.1m).
Propulsion: CODOG. Two Rolls-Royce Olympus TM3B gas turbines, 52,000shp; two SEMT-Pielstick 16PA6-CV280-BTC diesel, 10,400bhp; two shafts; 30kts.
Armament: Eight Exocet SSM (four only in first two ships); one Crotale Navale EDIR eight-cell SAM launcher; one 100mm Model 1968, DP gun; two Oerlikon 20mm AA cannon; two catapults for L-5 ASW torpedoes.
Aircraft: Two Westland WG-13 Lynx ASW helicopters.
ASW Sensors: D-640 to D-643. DUBV-23D hull-mounted sonar; DUBV-43B variable-depth sonar. D-644 to D-646. DUBV-24C hull-mounted sonar; DUBV-43B variable-depth sonar, DSBV-61 towed-array.
Complement: 216.

Below: Nameship of the class, *Georges Leygues* (D-640), at sea.

Above: *Montcalm* (D-642). In the second batch of four ships the bridge will be raised by one deck level, as the current design has proved too low, especially with sea breaking over the forecastle.

The French Navy has produced a very efficient hull design for the C70 class ships, which are being produced in two versions — the basic C70 or *Georges Leygues* class for ASW, and the C70AA (AA = 'anti-airienne') or *Cassard* class for air defence. Developed from the *Tourville* (F 67) class, the first of the ASW version was commissioned in 1979. The first four (*Georges Leygues, Deupleix, Montcalm* and *Jean de Vienne*) form the F 70 ASW (1) class and the remaining three (*Primauquet, Le Motte-Picquet* and *Latouche-Treville*) the F 70 ASW (2) class; a proposed eighth ship was cancelled as an economy measure. The main differences between the two versions are that the later group have a towed sonar array, in addition to the variable-depth sonar (VDS), and the bridge has been raised by one deck level to overcome the problems the first group experienced in bad weather.

All seven ships are fitted with a bow-mounted, low-frequency (LF) sonar: DUBV-23D in the first four and the essentially similar DUBV-24C in the last three. The array is mounted in a streamlined bulb and performs both search and attack functions. All seven ships have the DUBV-43C variable-depth sonar (VDS), in which the transducer array is mounted in a 'fish' streamed over the stern at distances of up to 820ft (250m) and at depths ranging from 33ft (10m) to 656ft (200m). Virtually all elements of the two systems are identical, apart from the transducer arrays and even they consist of essentially similar components. The fish also tows a tactical array (TACTASS) on a 640ft (200m) cable, while a second TACTASS is towed (3000m) astern of the ship at a depth of some 1600ft (500m). Towing all this gear naturally imposes limitations on the speed and manoeuvrability of these ships and the actual ASW attacks are undertaken by the Westland Lynx helicopter. The last three ships of the class are also fitted with the DSBV-61 passive, linear, towed array.

The principle ASW attack system is provided by two Westland WG.13 helicopters. These use the Sintra-Alcatel DUAV-4 dipping-sonar, which can operate at depths up to 495ft (148m) and are armed with US Honeywell Mk46 lightweight ASW torpedoes.

The first four ships (D-640 to D-643) operate in the Mediterranean and may be modernised to bring them up to the same standard as the last three in the mid-1990s. The remaining three ships serve in the Atlantic Fleet.

MEKO Class

Destroyers

12 ships: **Argentina** — four; **Nigeria** — one; **Portugal** — three; **Turkey** — four; (plus 14 building): **Australia** — eight; **Greece** — four; **New Zealand** — two.

Country of origin: Germany.
Displacement: 3,000 tons full load.
Dimensions: Length overall 362.5ft (110.5m); beam 43.6ft (13.3m); draught 12.8ft (3.9m).
Aircraft: One ASW helicopter (type varies).
Armament: Eight Harpoon SSM launchers; one Mk 29 launcher for Sea Sparrow SAMs; one 5in (127mm) Mk 45 DP gun; four 1in (25mm) GM Sea Zenith CIWS; six 12.7in (324mm) torpedo tubes.
Propulsion: Four MTU 20V1163 diesels (22,536shp); 27kts.
(Specifications are for Turkish MEKO 200; others differ in dimensions and weapons fit.)

One of the major dilemmas in modern naval construction is that warships are becoming ever more expensive and complex, while the growing size and ambitions of the world's smaller navies means that they want more of the latest types of warship — but within a limited budget. Several designers have, therefore, sought to produce warships of destroyer/frigate size which could accommodate a variety of weapons and electronic fits to suit different customers' needs on a common hull, which would result in longer production runs and reduced costs.

The basis of the MEKO concept, developed by Blohm & Voss in Germany,

is a range of standard hulls, complemented by the MEKO/FES range of standard-sized, functionally self-contained modules with standard interfaces to the ship platform. Weapon functional units are used for the installation of guns, missile launchers and ASW rocket launchers. These units are bedded into a unit foundation using a plastic resin compound which transfers the static and dynamic loads to the ship's structure. Among the units on offer are Otomat SAMs, Aspide SSMs, 5in (127mm) guns and twin 1.6in (40mm) Breda AA guns, but the system is so flexible that almost anything could be handled.

Largest in the current range is the MEKO 360, a general-purpose destroyer designed for world-wide operations under all climatic conditions. Five of these are in service: four with Argentina (*Almirante Brown, La Argentina, Heroina* and *Sarandi*), and one with Nigeria (*Aradu*).

The slightly smaller MEKO 200 is proving more popular. Four are already in service with the Turkish Navy (*Yavuz, Turgut Reis, Fatih* and *Yildirim*), of which two were built in Germany and two in Turkey, and another three joined the Portuguese fleet in 1990-91 (*Vasco da Gama, Alvares Cabral*, and *Corte Real*). A further 14 are now under construction for three other navies: Australia — eight; Greece — four; and New Zealand — two.

The German Navy has recently ordered a new class of large destroyer — the Type 123. This will displace 4,275 tons and is being constructed by a consortium led by Blohm & Voss. This design is somewhat larger than the current MEKO range, but uses the Blohm & Voss modular construction techniques developed for the MEKO ships and will clearly benefit greatly from the experience gained with these foreign orders. Meanwhile the MEKO destroyers must rank as some of the most successful designs currently in service.

Below: Commissioned on 26 January 1983, *Almirante Brown* (D 10) was sent to the Gulf in late-1990 to support Allied operations.

Giuseppe Garibaldi

Light fleet carrier
One carrier (C 551).

Country of origin: Italy.
Displacement: 10,100 tons standard (13,370 tons full load).
Dimensions: Length overall 591ft (180m); flight deck length 570.2ft (173.8m); beam 110.2ft (33.4m); draught 22ft (6.7m).
Aircraft: 16 McDonnell Douglas AV-8B Harrier II fighters; 18 Sikorsky SH-3D Sea King AEW/ASW helicopters.
Armament: Four OTO Melara missile launchers, two Selenia octuple launchers; six Breda 1.6in (40mm) guns. Six 12.7in (324mm) torpedo tubes firing Honeywell Mk 46 anti-submarine torpedoes.
Propulsion: Four Fiat gas turbines (80,000hp); 30 knots.

Below: A 6.5deg ski-jump set in the bows of the *Giuseppi Garibaldi* will enable AV-8B Harrier IIs to take off at higher gross weights. Up to 16 of these potent VSTOL fighters will be carried.

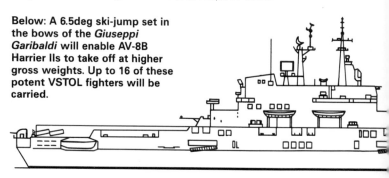

Below: A fine view of the integral ski-jump aboard the *Giuseppi Garibaldi,* with Royal Navy Sea Harriers on deck for launch trials.

Giuseppe Garibaldi is the first aircraft carrier to enter service with the Italian Navy. Previous examples utilizing converted liners during the Second World War were scuttled before they could be completed.

Authorized in late-1977, design work was not completed until early-1980 owing to extensive design changes. Laid down in March 1981, launched in June 1983 and commissioned in August 1987, the carrier has six decks with 13 water-tight bulkheads. A 6.5deg ski-jump for VSTOL aircraft forms part of the forward flight-deck, which in turn is served by two lifts leading to a 361ft x 49.2ft x 19.7ft (110m x 15m x 6m) hangar. By 1993, 16 AV-8B Harriers will be carried plus 18 SH-3D Sea King helicopters (twelve in the hangar and six on deck). Later these will be replaced by EH. 101s. The long-standing dispute between the Navy and Air Force concerning the former's operation of fixed-wing aircraft dates back prior to the Second World War and was not clarified until 1989, when it was decided that embarked aircraft were purchased and operated by the Navy with the Air Force providing maintenance, any evaluation and additional pilots if needed.

The first group of Navy pilots were trained in 1990-91 by the US Marine Corps. All defence is provided by six Breda 1.6in (40mm) AA guns plus four Melara active radar homing missiles and two Selenia Elsag Albatros octuple launchers with an envelope from only 49.2ft (15m) to 16,405ft (5,000m). There are also two triple torpedo mounts for anti-submarine defence.

Giuseppe Garibaldi has a range of 7000nm (13,300km) at 20kts.

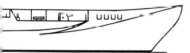

Below: A view of the *Giuseppi Garibaldi's* stern reveals one of the trio of Breda 1.6in (40mm) double-barrelled guns for anti-air and anti-surface defensive fire. Rate-of-fire is 300 rounds-per-minute, with an elevation of 85deg.

Maestrale Class

Frigates (Italy)

Eight ships

Displacement: 2,500 tons standard; 3040 tons full load.
Dimensions: Length overall 405ft (122·7m); beam 42·5ft (12·9m); draught (screws) 27·4ft (8·4m).
Propulsion: 2 Fiat gas turbines, 50,000shp; 2 diesels, 11,000bhp; 2 shafts; 32kt.
Armament: 4 Otomat Mk 2 SSM launchers; 1 5in (127mm) gun; 4 40mm guns; 2 triple Mk 32 torpedo tubes.
Aircraft: None.
ASW sensors: (Hull-mounted) DE-1164.
Complement: 232.

In the 1970s the Italian Navy built a successful class of 2,500-ton convoy escort frigates of the Lupo class. These have a respectable ASW armament of two triple Mk 32 torpedo tubes and a hangar for an ASW helicopter. Four were built for Italy and there have been a number of export orders: Iraq (4), Peru (4) and Venezuela (6). The Maestrale class, now under construction, has a superficial similarity to the Lupos but is, in fact, a new design to meet a new and different operational requirement for a fleet ASW escort. Obviously, however, the experience gained with the Lupos has been put to good effect in the new class.

ASW armament for *Maestrale* comprises two triple Mk 32 torpedo tubes for Mk 46 torpedoes, plus two fixed launchers for Whitehead Moto Fides A184 wire-guided torpedoes. The principal ASW sensor is the Raytheon DE-1164 integrated hull-mounted and variable-depth sonar. Finally, there is a flight deck and hangar for either one SH-3 Sea King or two AB 212 ASW helicopters. Surface armament comprises four Otomat Mk 2 SSMs and one 5in (127mm) gun in a DP mounting; air defence armament includes four 40mm automatic cannon and an Albatros launcher with eight Aspide SAMs.

Eight Maestrales have so far been ordered, all for the Italian Navy. The first was commissioned in February 1982 and the eighth will join the fleet in 1984.

Below: The Italian Navy's frigate *Maestrale* (F-570) at speed in the Tyrrhenian Sea. Eight of this class have been ordered, the last being due to join the fleet during 1984.

Vittorio Veneto Class

Guided-missile helicopter cruiser (Italy)
One ship

Displacement: 8,130 tons standard; 9,500 tons full load.
Dimensions: Length overall 589.2ft (179.6m); beam 63.7ft (19.42m); draught 18ft (5.5m).
Propulsion: Geared steam turbines, 73,000shp; 2 shafts; 30.5kts.
Armament: 1 twin Mk 20 launcher (60 Standard SM-1/ASROC missiles); 4 Otomat/Teseo Mk II SSM launchers; 8 3in (76mm) guns; 6 1.6in (40mm) guns; 2 triple Mk 32 12.7in (324mm) torpedo tubes.
ASW sensors: (Hull-mounted) SQS-23.
Complement: 550.

Above: The sole vessel in her class, *Vittorio Veneto* officially serves the Italian Navy as a guided-missile helicopter cruiser. Up to six AB.212 ASW helicopters can be accommodated onboard.

Vittorio Veneto is the third in a series of Italian air-capable ASW cruisers completed in the 1960s; *Andrea Doria* and *Caio Duilio* are smaller and operate only four AB.204 ASW helicopters with a conventional large double hangar. In *Vittorio Veneto* these arrangements are much modified: there is an extra deck aft with a large hangar beneath it; and there are four helicopter spots on the capacious flight-deck, which is served by a large centreline lift. *Vittorio Veneto* was designed to operate nine AB.204 helicopters, but these have now been superceded by six AB.212s (qv), with an alternative complement of four licence-built ASH-3 Sea Kings.

In a 1981-83 refit, *Vittorio Veneto's* armament was revised: the Terrier missile system was upgraded to fire the Standard SM-1 (ER) missile, and the single 76mm was replaced by three twin 40mm/70 Breda compact mountings with Dardo fire control systems; four Otomat Mk2 SSMs were also fitted. On-board ASW equipment remains a hull-mounted SQS-23 sonar and two triple Mk 32 torpedo tubes firing Mk 46 torpedoes.

Vittorio Veneto is a handsome and effective warship, and well suited for the prime role of ASW in a Mediterranean environment. Like the *Andrea Doria* class, she lacks a powerful surface weapon, but, like them, she is designed to operate as part of a task force.

Shirane/Haruna Classes

Destroyers (Japan)
Two/two ships

Displacement: 5,200 tons standard; 6,800 tons full load.
Dimensions: Length overall 521ft (158.8m); beam 57.5ft (17.5m); draught 17.5ft (5.3m).
Propulsion: Geared steam turbines, 70,000shp; 2 shafts; 32kt.
Armament: 1 octuple ASROC Mk 16 launcher; 2 single 5in (127mm) Mk 42 guns; 1 Sea Sparrow SAM launcher; 2 Phalanx CIWS; 2 triple Mk 32 torpedo tubes.
Aircraft: 3 HSS-2B Sea King.
ASW sensors: (Hull-mounted) OQS-101 SQS-35 (J); (towed array) SQR-18.
Complement: 350.
(Specifications given for Shirane class; see text for details of Haruna class.)

The CIS Navy's Pacific Fleet is based at Vladivostok, Sovetskaya Gavan and Petropavlovsk-Kamchatskiy, none of which have direct access to the ocean. It is Japan's misfortune to sit astride most of the exits, as well as being the only non-Russian navy with access to the Sea of Okhotsk. Mindful of the large submarine component of the CIS Navy, the Japanese Maritime Self-Defence Force (JMSDF) has built up a naval element with a primary ASW role. Its surface ships are of Japanese design and construction, but tend to use weapons systems and armament of US origin, either locally manufactured under licence or purchased directly. The showpieces of the fleet are the four helicopter-carrying

Below: The Japanese MSDF has built up a useful ASW force of surface ships, one class being the Shirane, with the nameship of the class shown here. Visible to the rear is an HSS-2B Sea King landing on.

ASW destroyers of the Haruna and Shirane classes; the former were completed in 1973-74 and the latter in 1980-81. No further vessels are planned for either class.

Both classes have a very large hangar which accommodates three Mitsubishi HSS-2B (licence-built Sikorsky Sea King) helicopters. The spacious flight deck extends to the stern, and incorporates the Canadian 'Beartrap' haul-down system. Both classes have an ASROC launcher forward of the bridge and Mk 46 torpedo tubes in two triple mountings abreast the bridge. Hull sonars of Japanese design and manufacture are fitted (OQS-3 in Haruna; OQS-101 in Shirane). Shirane currently is the only class to have SQS-35 VDS. The Shiranes also have SQR-18 TACTASS towed arrays. Surface armament includes two quick-firing 5in (127mm) Mk 42 guns in all four ships, complemented by BPDMS and Phalanx CIWS in the Shirane class. Although it was not originally fitted, an octuple Raytheon Mk 29 Sea Sparrow SAM launcher was installed in the two Harunas during a refit in the 1980s.

These are two classes of impressive and capable ships, in the best Japanese maritime traditions. The JMSDF will soon have a surface fleet of thirty five destroyers and eighteen frigates, all of which will be optimised for the highly important ASW role.

Below: The Haruna class of two ships preceded the Shirane class and is very similar.

Kortenaer Class

Frigates (Netherlands)
Ten ships

Displacement: 3,786 tons full load.
Dimensions: Length overall 427.2ft (130.2m); beam 47.2ft (14.4m); draught 14.3ft (4.4m).
Propulsion: Two Rolls-Royce Olympus TM-3B gas turbines, 50,000shp; two Rolls-Royce tyne RM-1C gas turbines (8,000shp); two shafts; 30kts.
Armament: Four Harpoon SSM; one NATO Sea Sparrow SAM system; one 76mm OTO Melara DP; one 30mm Goalkeeper CIWS; four 324mm torpedo tubes.
Aircraft: Two Westland WG13 Lynx helicopters.
ASW sensors: First six — one SQS-505; last four — one SQS-509.
Complement: 200.

Between 1975 and 1983 the Royal Netherlands Navy undertook a fundamental reorganization in which it created an integrated and balanced force consisting of three ASW task groups in war. Each would comprise a flagship/air defence ship, six ASW frigates and a logistic support vessel and would be allocated to NATO. To achieve this a new class of frigates was required to augment and eventually replace the *Van Speijk* class, which were Dutch-built versions of the British *Leander* class. The result was the *Kortenaer* class, which has proved an outstanding success.

Displacing 3,786tons, the *Kortenaer* is one of the larger frigates in service and is well armed. For surface warfare there are four Harpoon SSM launchers (a further four can be carried in war) and a single 76mm OTO Melara DP gun, one of the most widely used naval guns in the world. Air defence weapons comprise the NATO Sea Sparrow system, for which 29 missiles are carried, and a Dutch-designed Goalkeeper 30mm CIWS (not yet fitted to all ships in the class).

For the ASW mission a large hangar can accommodate two Westland Lynx helicopterss, although in peacetime only one is normally carried. Primary ASW sensor is the Canadian SQS-505, which is also used in the Canadian *Iroquois* and *Halifax* classes and in the Belgian *Wielingen* class frigates. There is no towed array, nor are there any known plans to fit one.

All the Dutch ships were launched between 1976 and 1981, and the last six to be completed will undergo a limited modernization from 1992 onwards. The remaining four will not be modernized and will be placed in reserve in 1996.

Germany has built seven of these ships as the *Bremen* (Type 122) class, which are generally similar to the Dutch ships, but are modified for operations in the Baltic and are powered by Ge-Fiat gas turbines and MTU diesels, in a CODOG arrangement. The Greek Navy operates two Dutch-built Kortenaer class.

Below: The *Elli*, one of the Greek Navy Kortenaers.

Tromp Class

Destroyers (Netherlands)

Two ships

Displacement: 3,900 tons standard; 4,580 tons full load.
Dimensions: Length overall 454·1ft (138·4m); beam 48·6ft (14·8m); draught 15·1ft (4·6m).
Propulsion: 2 Rolls-Royce Olympus gas turbines, 50,000shp; 2 Rolls-Royce Tyne cruising gas turbines, 8,000shp; 2 shafts; 30kt.
Armament: 8 Harpoon SSM launchers; 1 Tartar Mk 13 SAM launcher; 2 quadruple Sea Sparrow SAM launchers; 1 twin 4·7in (120mm) gun; 2 triple Mk 32 torpedo tubes.
Aircraft: 1 WG13 Lynx.
ASW sensors: (Hull-mounted) CWE-610.
Complement: 246.

It is the Dutch intention to create an integrated, efficient and balanced fleet, at the heart of which will be three task forces each comprising a flagship, six ASW frigates and a logistic support vessel. Two of these forces will be allocated to CINCEASTLANT and one to CINCHAN. Two of the three flagships will be *Tromp* and *De Ruyter*, one of the finest designs of recent years. Their armament is particularly heavy, with a twin 4·7in (120mm) turret, Sea Sparrow BPDMS, Standard Tartar SAM and Harpoon SSMs. Two of the major visual features are the high bridge, surmounted by the enormous Hollandse Signaalapparat radome, and the bifurcated uptakes. Triple Mk 32 torpedo tubes are mounted either side of the after superstructure, firing Mk 46 torpedoes. Refits for these two ships are planned for 1984–86.

The remaining ships in the three Dutch task forces, apart from the Kortenaers described below, will be six frigates of the Van Speijk class. These are Dutch-built, somewhat modified versions of the British Leander class; all have recently completed mid-life refits and will continue to serve for the foreseeable future.

The Tromp class represent the upper end of the type of all-round destroyer/frigate which the smaller navies can afford to build. The success of the Dutch concepts was not, however, to come with the Tromps, good as they are, but with the next class, which incorporates all the lessons learned—the Kortenaers.

Below: The unmistakable profile of a Tromp class frigate. The huge radome houses a Hollandse Signaalapparat 3-dimensional radar antenna. Designed as flagships for the Dutch task forces operating under NATO command in war, these two ships represent one of the most outstanding postwar surface warship designs.

Al Madinah Class

Frigates (Saudi Arabia)
Four ships

Displacement: 2,000 tons standard; 2,610 tons full load.
Dimensions: Length overall 377.3ft (115.0m); beam 41.0ft (12.5m); draught 11.2ft (3.4m).
Propulsion: 4 SEMT-Pielstick 16 PA6-BTC diesels, 32,500bhp; 2 shafts; 30kt.
Armament: 2 quadruple Otomat Mk2 SSM launchers; 1 octuple Crotale EDIR SAM launcher; 1 3.9in (100mm) DP gun; 4 1.57in (40mm) AA guns; 4 21in (533mm) tubes for F17 ASW torpedoes.
Aircraft: One Aerospatiale Dauphin 2 ASW helicopter.
ASW Sensors: (Hull-mounted) Thompson-CSF TSM 2630 (Diodon); (VDS) TSM 2630 (Sorel).
Complement: 179.

The Kingdom of Saudi Arabia has long been the richest of the Arab states, but only in the past 20 years has it sought to assert military power as well. The navy had some 10,000 officers and men in 1991, while hardware comprised mainly smaller warships. The USA was the kingdom's principle naval supplier until the placing of the contract for the Al Madinah class frigates with France in 1980.

These are not copies of any existing French design, but seem to represent a type of ship that the French Navy would have liked if it had the same bottomless purse as Saudi Arabia! The Al Madinah class are very well appointed and include much new, state-of-the-art equipment. The Otomat anti-ship missiles are the Mark 2 version, but with the French-developed Extended Range Targetting of Otomat, or ERATO feature, for which a Dauphin 2 helicopter is carried to give mid-course guidance. This system can handle up to 16 missiles attacking six targets simultaneously.

The main ASW weapons are French F17 wire-guided torpedoes. The four tubes are mounted on the quarter-deck, facing aft. In this way the wires pay out as the ship steams away. The torpedoes have a range of 22,000 yards (20,000m) and a speed of 40 knots.

Al Madinah, the first-of-class, arrived in Saudi waters in July 1985 and the fourth and last, *Taif*, in January 1987.

Above: Saudi Arabia's Al Madinah class frigates are much-improved versions of previous French designs, and were in fact built at French yards between 1981 and 1983. All the Al Madinah class are based in the Red Sea. This is the *Al Madinah*. Others in the class include *Hofouf, Abha* and *Taif*.

Left: An excellent view of the *Al Madinah*'s weapons and radar array. The F17 ASW torpedoes are located at the stern, behind the helipad, while the EDIR SAM launcher can be seen on top of the hangar for the Dauphin 2 helicopter. The Mk 2 Otomat missiles are located amidships.

Principe de Asturias Class

Aircraft carrier
One ship (R 11).

Country of origin: Spain.
Displacement: 16,700 tons full load.
Dimensions: Length overall 642ft (195m); beam 79.7ft (24.3m); draught 30.8ft (9.4m).
Aircraft: Six to 12 McDonnell Douglas AV-8B Harrier II fighters; six to 10 Sikorsky SH-3D/G Sea King, two Sikorsky SH-60B Seahawk and two to four Agusta-Bell AB.212ASW helicopters.
Armament: Four Bazan Meroka 12-barrelled 0.8in (20mm) anti-missile guns; two Rheinmetall 1.45in (37mm) saluting guns.
Propulsion: Two gas-turbines; one shaft; 26kts.

After negotiating considerable financial and technical assistance from the United States, Spain ordered a replacement for the ageing 13,000-ton *Dëdalo* in June 1977. The basic design comes from the US Sea Control Ship study of early-1974, but with considerable refinements such as two lifts, one of which is offset to starboard ahead of the island which is placed well aft. The second lift is positioned on the centreline at the after flight-deck edge. A modified flight-deck, which is partly axial, allows for a conventional take-off run by the fixed-wing AV-8B V/STOL aircraft culminating in an integrally structured "ski-jump", so enabling the aircraft to be launched with greater loads. Deck parking is usually on the starboard side aft.

The small island incorporates the command centre and the funnel uptakes. It also houses the only defensive battery of four 12-barrelled Meroka anti-missile guns plus the sea and air radar search and fire control systems.

Laid down at Ferrol in October 1979 and launched in May 1982, *Principe de Asturias* (R 11) was not commissioned until six years later owing to major changes to the command and control systems and the addition of a bridge.

Six to 12 AV-8B Harrier II fixed-wing aircraft plus six to ten SH-3 Sea Kings and up to six SH-60B Seahawk helicopters are carried. The maximum effective operational number of aircraft that can be carried is 24, but by parking on deck up to 37 can be catered for if the need arises. The below deck hangar is nearly 25,000sq ft (2,340m²) in area.

Below: Unlike aircraft carriers in other small navies, Spain's *Principe de Asturias* (R 11) is modern and custom-built for her mission. She is powered by two General Electric gas-turbines.

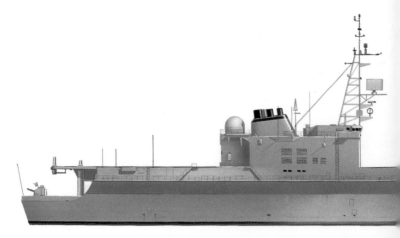

Above: With Italy's *Giuseppe Garibaldi* (C 551) to starboard, *Principe de Asurias* (R 11) cruises in the Mediterranean Sea.

Below: Between six to 12 McDD AV-8B Harrier II V/STOL fighters are embarked aboard the Spanish Navy's aircraft carrier when at sea.

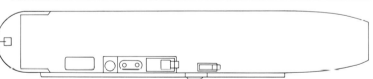

Above: A plan-view before the installation of the "ski-jump".

Amazon Class

Frigates (UK)
Six ships

Displacement: 2,750 tons standard; 3,250 tons full load.
Dimensions: Length overall 384ft (117m); beam 40.5ft (12.3m); draught 19ft (5.8m).
Propulsion: 2 Rolls-Royce Olympus gas turbines, 56,000shp; 2 Rolls-Royce Tyne gas turbines, 8,500shp; 2 shafts; 30kt.
Armament: 4 Exocet SSM launchers; 1 4.5in (114mm) gun; 4 0.8in (20mm) AA guns; 2 triple 12.75in (324mm) torpedo tubes.
Aircraft: Westland Lynx.
ASW sensors: (Hull-mounted) Type 184M sonar.
Complement: 177.

Before the first of the 'broad-beamed' Leander class frigates had been laid down, Vosper-Thornycroft received a contract for a new design to be prepared in collaboration with Yarrow Shipbuilders Ltd. They produced the Type 21 Amazon class, the first being launched in 1971 and commissioned in 1974. These were the first Royal Navy ships to be designed from the outset to be powered solely by gas turbines, and were also the first for many years to be designed by a commercial firm.

The ASW fit includes a Type 184M hull-mounted sonar, and the ASW armament comprises two triple torpedo tubes for Mk 48 torpedoes; the ships also have

a flight deck and hangar for the Westland HAS.3 Lynx ASW helicopter. Other armament includes a 4.5in (114mm) main gun in a DP mounting, four Exocet SSMs and four 20mm Oerlikon cannon. Despite this heavy armament (relative to the hull size), the complement of each vessel in the class is only 177 officers and ratings.

Each of the Amazons has some 135 tons of aluminium alloy in its structure and the spectacular destruction of HMS' *Amazon* and *Antelope* during the South Atlantic War led to reports that it was the aluminium that was responsible. This was investigated fully after the war and the chairman of the working party stated that he was 'not aware of any evidence to suggest that any ship was lost because of the use of aluminium alloys in its construction. Nor was there any evidence that aluminium or aluminium alloys had burned' (*Financial Times*, 24 December 1982).

These are handsome ships that have served the Royal Navy well, and it is indeed sad that two out of the eight should have been lost in a war. It is also worth noting that no fewer than seven out of the eight in the class were in the Falklands area during the war. The surviving six ships are assigned to the Royal Navy's 4th Frigate Squadron.

Below: The Amazon Class frigates have undergone a series of modifications to their hulls, due partly to structural defects in the upper deck, and to recurrent problems with noise and vibration. These modifications, however, should be completed in all six ships by the end of 1992.

Broadsword (Type 22) Class

General-purpose frigates
16 ships: **United Kingdom** — 14 (**Batch 1** — four (F 88-F 91); **Batch 2** —
six (F 92-F 96, F 98); **Batch 3** — four (F 85-F 87, F 99)); **Argentina** — two
(D 1-D 2).

Country of origin: United Kingdom.
Displacement: Batch 1 — 4,400 tons; **Batches 2/3** — 4,850 tons.
Dimensions: Length (**Batch 1**) — 430.4ft (131.2m); **Batches 2/3** — 485.9ft
(148.1m). Beam (all) 48.69ft (14.8m). Draught (**Batches 1/2**) 14.1ft (4.3m),
Batch 3 — 17.7ft (5.4m).
Aircraft: Batch 1 — one Westland Lynx; **Batch 2** — one/two Westland
Lynx HAS.3; **Batch 3** — two Westland Lynx or one Westland Sea King.
Armament: Batches 1/2 — four MM38 Exocet SSM; two Sea Wolf
GWS.25 SAM; two 1.6in (40mm) Mk 9 AA; six 12.7in (324mm) ASW
torpedo tubes; **Batch 3** — eight Harpoon SSM launchers; two Sea Wolf
GWS.25 Mod 3 SAM systems; one 4.5in (114mm) Vickers Mk 8 DP gun;
one 1.12in (30mm) Goalkeeper CIWS; two 1.12 (30mm) DS-30B AA; six
12.7in (324mm) STWS.2 ASW torpedo tubes.
Propulsion: Batch 1 plus first two of **Batch 2** — COGOG. Two Olympus
TM38 gas-turbines (27,300shp each); two Tyne RM1A gas-turbines,
(4,100shp); two shafts; 29kts; **Batch 2** (last four) and **Batch 3** — COGAG.
Two Rolls-Royce Spey SM.1A DR gas-turbines, (18,770shp each); two Rolls-
Royce Tyne RM.1C gas-turbines (5,340shp each); two shafts; 30kts.

Following its very successful Leander class, the Royal Navy designed a successor, the Type 22 ASW frigate, the class taking its name from the first to be launched (12 May 1975): HMS *Broadsword* (F 88). Displacing 4,400 tons, it was planned to build 26 of these ships, which were armed with Sea Wolf SAMs, MM38 Exocet SSMs and ASW torpedo tubes, but lacking any form of gun. Their principle ASW system was the Lynx helicopter. HMS *Broadsword* entered service in 1979, by which time it had already been decided to modify the design by lengthening the hull, which was required to improve seaworthiness and endurance, and to provide extra space for additional weapons and sensors. This resulted in the Boxer (or Type 22 Batch 2) class, the first four ships then being redesignated Batch 1. One of the many lessons of the Falklands War was that guns were still necessary, but it was too late to incorporate any in the Batch 2 ships, although most, but not all, now mount two 1.12 (30mm) AA cannon. Six were built, of which HMS *Sheffield* (F 96) and HMS *Coventry* (F 98) were replacements for the Type 42 destroyers lost in the Falklands War.

The Batch 3 ships use the same hull as the Batch 2s, but with the weapons systems rearranged so that a 4.5in (114mm) gun can be mounted on the forecastle. The Exocet SSMs have been replaced by Harpoons, which are mounted abaft the bridge. In addition, a Dutch Goalkeeper CIWS has been mounted immediately before the mast.

The only overseas orders placed for this class were for two Batch 1 ships by the Argentine Navy. The first, *Hercules*, was built in Britain and entered service in 1976, while the second, *Santissima Trinidad*, was built in Argentina.

Below: HMS *Brave* (F 94), the third Batch 2 frigate, was laid down in 1982, launched in 1983, and commissioned in 1986.

Duke (Type 23) Class

General-purpose frigates
Four ships (F 229-F 231, F 233); six building (F 234-F 239).

Country of origin: United Kingdom.
Displacement: 4,200 tons full load.
Dimensions: Length overall 436.4ft (133.0m); beam 52.8ft (16.1m); draught 14.1ft (4.3m).
Aircraft: One West and Lynx or (from mid-1990s) Agusta-Westland EH.101 Merlin ASW helicopter.
Armament: Eight Harpoon SSM launchers; one Seawolf SAM vertical launch group; one 4.5in (114mm) Mk 8 DP gun; two 1.12in (30mm) DS-30B AA cannon; four 12.7in (324mm) ASW torpedo tubes.
Propulsion: CODLAG: two Rolls-Royce Spey SMIA gas-turbines; four Paxman Valenta 12 RPA 200CZ diesel generator sets; two electric motors (41,250shp); two shafts; 28kts.

The Royal Navy's Duke (Type 23) class frigates were planned as the successor to the very successful Leander class, 25 of which were built between 1960 and 1973. Design work started in the late-1970s and was progressing well when the Falklands War took place. A major consequence of the lessons learned from the naval campaign (where the Royal Navy lost three warships) was that a major redesign became necessary and the ship's size increased considerably to accommodate the changes. At one stage it was planned to build at least 17, but the final figure is now uncertain, in view of the British Defence cuts resulting from the end of the Cold War. Ten were on order in late-1991, of which the first, HMS *Norfolk*, was commissioned in July 1989 followed by HMS *Marlborough* in 1990, and HMS *Argyll* and HMS *Lancaster* in 1991, with the remaining seven scheduled to join the fleet between 1992 and 1995.

The Duke class design is unusual in Royal Navy practice in having a flush-decked hull and a large angular stack, instead of the usual well-rounded design. It also has the first bow sonar to be fitted in a Royal Navy ship, all previous installations having been hull-mounted. There is a large hangar and the flight-deck is fitted, again for the first time in a British warship, with a haul-down system. The current ASW helicopter is the West and Lynx, but this will be replaced by the Anglo-Italian EH 101 Merlin when it enters service.

The propulsion system is most unusual, being CODLAG — Combined Diesel Electric and Gas-turbine. Each of the electric propulsion motors is built around one of the shafts and can be powered by any combination of the diesel generators. These are used for quiet running, especially when hunting submarines, giving speeds of up to 15kts. For higher speeds the gas-turbines are switched in. The propellers are fixed-pitch and astern drive can only be obtained using the two electric motors.

Main armament is concentrated on the foredeck. There is a single Vickers 4.5in (114mm) DP gun, behind which is a deckhouse/magazine containing the vertical launch tubes for the Sea Wolf SAM system, which has proved its effectiveness in both the Falklands and Gulf Wars. Between this and the bridge are the eight Harpoon SSM tubes, four firing on either beam.

Considerable efforts have been made to reduce the ships' radar signature. All upright surfaces are sloped at 7deg, edges are rounded and infra-red emissions have been reduced as far as is practicable.

A surprising omission is a CIWS gun, such as a Dutch Goalkeeper. However, there is some discussion of lengthening the hull in later ships (as has been done with the later batches of both Types 22 and 42). This would permit an increase in the size of the Sea Wolf VLS and the fitting of at least one Goalkeeper.

Below: Destined to form a major element within the Royal Navy of the 1990s and beyond, the Duke class frigate incorporates much stealth technology to reduce acoustic, magnetic, radar and infra-red signatures. Illustrated is HMS *Norfolk* (F 230).

Invincible Class

Light aircraft carriers
Three ships (R 05-R 07).

Country of origin: United Kingdom.
Displacement: 20,600 tons.
Dimensions: Length 689ft (210m); beam 118.1ft (36m); draught 21.3ft (6.5m).
Aircraft: Nine BAe Sea Harrier FRS.1; three Westland Sea King Mk.2A AEW and nine Westland Sea King HAS.Mk 6 ASW helicopters.
Armament: One Sea Dart GWS.30 Mod 2 SAM system; **HMS *Invincible*** — three 1.12in (30mm) Goalkeeper CIWS; **HMS *Illustrious*** — two 0.8in (20mm) Mk15 CIWS; **HMS *Ark Royal*** — three 0.8in (20mm) Mk15 CIWS; four Sea Wolf GWS.26 Mod 2 lightweight SAM systems (after current refits); two 0.8in (20mm) GAM-B01 AA guns.
Propulsion: Four Rolls-Royce Olympus TM.3B gas-turbines (112,000shp); two shafts; 28kts.

Below: An excellent illustration of HMS *Invincible* (R 05) while on manoeuvres. Visible on deck is a Seak King helicopter and a pair of Sea Harrier fighters. The latter make full use of the "ski-jump".

Following the 1960s political decision to cancel the proposed attack carrier (*CVA-01*), design work started on a new type of large, air-capable, ASW cruiser, intended for deployment into NATO's Eastern Atlantic (EASTLANT) area of operations. The design went through a series of changes in response to both political and naval manoeuvring in the British Ministry of Defence, one facet of which was the somewhat transparent attempt to disguise the ships' purpose by describing them as "through-deck cruisers", rather than as "aircraft carriers". Originally intended only to operate large ASW helicopters, late design changes had to be made to enable them to operate Sea Harrier fighters as well.

The Invincible class has an open forecastle head deck enabling them to mount a twin-arm Sea Dart SAM launcher, supplemented, as a result of experience in the Falklands War, by a CIWS: a Dutch Goalkeeper in the case of HMS *Invincible* and a Mk15 Phalanx in the other two. The other CIWS are mounted in various positions in the three ships. All ships also have a twin 0.8in (20mm) GAM-BO1

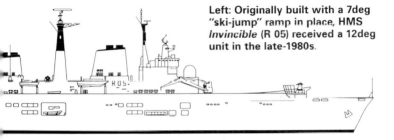

Left: Originally built with a 7deg "ski-jump" ramp in place, HMS *Invincible* (R 05) received a 12deg unit in the late-1980s.

Leander Class

Frigates (UK)
Thirty-five ships

Displacement: 2,500 tons standard; 2,962 tons full load.
Dimensions: Length overall 372ft (113.4m); beam 43ft (13.1m); draught 18ft (5.5m).
Propulsion: 2 geared turbines, 30,000shp; 2 shafts; 28kt.
Armament: 4 MM 38 Exocet launchers; 1 6-barrelled Seawolf GWS 25 Mod 0 launcher; 4 0.8in (20mm) guns; 2 triple 12.75in (324mm) torpedo tubes.
Aircraft: 1 Lynx ASW helicopter.
ASW sensors: (Hull-mounted) Type 162M, Type 2016.
Complement: 260.
(Specifications are for Batch 3A ships.)

The first unit of the very successful Leander class was laid down on 10 April 1959 and commissioned on 27 March 1963. The class was the first Royal Navy design to include a helicopter and represents the largest single group of ships to be built for the Royal Navy for many years. The ships were designed specifically for ASW duties and carried a hull-mounted sonar, stern-mounted VDS (since removed) and a variety of ASW weapons. The last ten of the class were 2ft (0.6m) broader to improve stability, and have become known, somewhat inelegantly, as the 'broad-beamed' Leanders.

A whole series of conversions has taken place. These involved fitting either the Ikara ASW system or Exocet SSMs, both at the expense of the twin 4.5in (114mm) gun mounting, a step which was to be regretted following the South Atlantic War of 1982.

Some fifty Leanders were built in Australia (two), India (six), the Netherlands (six) and the UK (twenty-seven, of which two were for Chile) between 1961 and 1981. Of these, some have been scrapped and others transferred. In 1992 thirty-five remained in service: RN — fourteen; Australia — two, Chile — three; India — six; Indonesia — six; and New Zealand — four.

Above: HMS *Scylla* (F 71) of the broad-beamed Leander class cruising through disputed waters off the coast of Iceland in 1973 during the confrontation over the extent of fishing waters which became popularly known as the "Cod War". She was improved and modified in 1984 and is now substantially better-armed with Exocet SSMs, Seawolf SAMs, four 20mm Oerlikon guns and torpedoes.

Left: HMS *Andromeda* (F 57), is a member of the five-strong Batch 3A Conversion group of broad-beamed Leanders which includes *Scylla*. She is seen here after her armaments and electronics refit. The marked deck for the Westland Lynx HAS 3 ASW helicopter is clearly visible. Note the Macroni Type 967/968 air/surface search radar atop the mast and the six-barrelled launcher for Seawolf surface-to-air missiles on the forward deck.

Knox Class

Frigates (USA)
Forty-six frigates

Displacement: 3,075 tons standard; 4,260 tons full load.
Dimensions: Length overall 438ft (133.5m); beam 46.8ft (14.3m); draught 15ft (4.6m).
Propulsion: 1 geared turbine, 35,000shp; 1 shaft; 27kt.
Armament: 1 Mk 112 launcher for Harpoon and ASROC missiles; 1 5in (127mm) Mk 42 DP gun; 1 0.8in (20mm) Mk 15 CIWS; 4 fixed Mk 32 torpedo tubes.
Aircraft: 1 SH-2F Seasprite LAMPS-I ASW helicopter.
ASW sensors: (Hull-mounted) SQS-26; (VDS) SQS-35.
Complement: 25.

The Knox class began as a design for a missile escort, but Congressional opposition led to it being redesigned as an ASW escort. Although it retains the one-shaft propulsion system of the Garcia/Brooke design, the complicated pressure-fired boilers of the latter were abandoned in favour of a safer, more conventional steam plant. This resulted in an increase in size without creating any extra space for weapons or sensors.

Above: USS *Stein*, fourteenth of the forty-six Knox class frigates.

The armament provides a first-class ASW outfit. There is an eight-cell Mk 112 launcher on the foredeck; six cells are used for ASROC and the port pair for Harpoon SSMs. Both types of missile can be reloaded from the magazine beneath the bridge. Aft is a hangar with a telescopic extension for a LAMPS-I ASW helicopter.

All ships have retained the original, hull-mounted SQS-26 sonar and all but eleven were later fitted with the SQS-35 VDS and, later still, with SQR-18A TACTASS towed array. Most ships in the class were fitted at one time with Sea Sparrow SAM launchers, but these have been replaced by a single 0.8in (20mm) Mk 15 CIWS.

Forty-six Knox class frigates were built for the USN, of which one was lost in an accident. In 1991 the US Navy decided not to update their ships and many are being transferred to the reserve, while some are being sold abroad.

Left: USS *Roark* was the second Knox class ship. Designed to operate the DASH ASW helicopter drone, these frigates were subsequently modified to operate the Kaman SH-2 Seasprite LAMPS-I helicopter.

Below: The clean and simple lines of the Knox class design can be seen to good effect in this view of USS *Harold E. Holt*. Behind the foredeck 5in (127mm) gun is the Harpoon/ASROC octuple launcher.

Oliver Hazard Perry (FFG 7) Class

Guided-missile frigates
USA — 51 (FFG 7-FFG 16, FFG 19-FFG 34, FFG 36-FFG 43, FFG 45-FFG 61); **Australia** — five (01-05), one building (06); **Spain** — four (F 81-F 84), two building (F 85-F 86); **Taiwan** — 12 building.

Country of origin: United States.
Displacement: 3,658 tons (short hull), 4,100 tons (long hull).
Dimensions: Length overall (short hull) 444.9ft (135.6m), (long hull) 455.4ft (138.8m); beam 44.9ft (13.7m); draught 19ft (5.8m).
Aircraft: One Kaman SH-2F Seasprite LAMPS I helicopter (short hull), one/two Sikorsky SH-60B Seahawk LAMPS III helicopter (long hull).
Armament: One Mk 13 Mod 4 launcher for Harpoon SSM and Standard SM-1 MR SAM; one 3in (76mm) Mk 75 DP gun, one 0.8in (20mm) Mk 15 gatling CIWS; six 12.7in (324mm) ASW torpedo tubes.
Propulsion: Two GE LM-2500 gas-turbines; one shaft; 29kts.

The Oliver Hazard Perry (FFG 7) class was designed in the early-1970s as the cheaper component of a high/low technology mix and was intended to provide a large number of escorts with reduced capabilities and thus reduced price. These were intended to balance the very expensive, specialized ASW and AAW ships needed to protect carriers, and strict limits were placed on cost, displacement and manpower.

These ships have been built in smaller yards, utilizing simpler construction techniques, making maximum use of flat panels and bulkheads, and keeping internal passageways as straight as possible. Propulsion is by two gas-turbines, but, as with earlier US frigates there is only one propeller. One unusual feature is that two small, retractable "propulsion pods" are fitted to provide emergency "get-you-home" power and to assist in docking; each pod has a 325hp engine and both can propel the ship at about 6kts.

The single Mk 13 launcher arm on the foredeck can launch either Standard SAMs (36 carried) or Harpoon SSMs (4 carried). A 3in (76mm) Mk 75 gun turret

Below: An example of strength in depth, with a trio of Oliver Hazard Perry class frigates on patrol. In the foreground is USS *Jack Williams* (FFG 24), flanked by USS *Antrim* (FFG 20) and the first-of-class, USS *Oliver Hazard Perry* (FFG 7).

licence-built OTO Melara Compact) is atop the superstructure just forward of a very abbreviated stack. A 0.8in (20mm) Mk 15 CIWS is mounted on the roof of the hangar. ASROC is not carried and the only ASW weapons on the ship are two triple 12.7in (324mm) torpedo tubes.

The flight-deck and hangar can handle a Kaman SH-2F Seasprite LAMPS I helicopter, but not the newer and more effective Sikorsky SH-60B Seahawk LAMPS III. This problem was solved in a neat and economic manner by angling out the transom to 45deg, which extends the overall length of the ship by 10.4ft (3.16m) without altering the waterline length, and enables a Recovery Assistance, Securing and Traversing system (RAST) to be fitted. Other modifications were also made, including fitting fin stablizers. This new layout was trialled aboard USS *McInerny* (FFG 8) and then incorporated as standard during construction into USS *Underwood* (FFG 36) and subsequent ships. It is also being fitted into some of the earlier ships during refits.

These ships have proved to be very capable in service and are actually used more as general-purpose destroyers than as "escorts". As a result they have had much extra equipment put in and, despite a design full load displacement of 3,600 tons with a 39 tons growth margin, they now displace some 4,100 tons at full load! Many have served in the Gulf, where USS *Stark* (FFG 31) was hit by two Exocets (one of which did not explode) and another, USS *Samuel B. Roberts* (FFG 58) hit a mine; both survived, returned to the USA for repairs and are now back in service.

The design has proved popular abroad. Four were built in the USA for the Royal Australian Navy with a further two now under construction in Australia itself. Another six are being built by Bazan for the Spanish Navy (Santa Maria class), with a probability of another six to replace the cancelled NATO NFR90 project. Finally, Taiwan is building six to the standard design (PFG-2-I class) and six to a modified design (PFG-2-II class) incoporating a 17ft (5.18m) plug and considerably modified armament.

Right: The foredeck of the Oliver Hazard Perry class frigate design is dominated by the single Mk 13 Mod 4 SAM/SSM launcher unit.

Below: The unusual profile of the superstructure is shown to good effect in this view of USS *Oliver Hazard Perry* (FFG 7).

Spruance Class

Destroyers
31 ships (DD 963-DD 992, DD 997).

Country of origin: United States.
Displacement: 8,040 tons.
Dimensions: Length overall 563.3ft (171.7m); beam 55.1ft (16.8m); draught 19.0ft (5.8m).
Aircraft: One Kaman SH-2F Seasprite LAMPS I or one Sikorsky SH-60B Seahawk LAMPS III ASW helicopter.
Armament: Seven ships (**DDs 974, 976, 979, 983-984, 989-990**): two Mk 44 quad box launchers for eight BGM-109 Tomahawk SLCM; two quad launchers for eight RGM-84A Harpoon SSM; six Mk 32 12.7in (324mm) tubes for 14 Mk 46 torpedoes (to be replaced by Mk 50 torpedoes); one Mk 29 octuple launcher for 24 Sea Sparrow SAM; 24 Mk 16 octuple launchers for ASROC; two Mk 45 Mod 0/1 5in (127mm) guns, two Mk 15 Vulcan Phalanx 0.8in (20mm) CIWS; four 0.5in (12.7mm) machine-guns. **All others:** as above except Mk 44 launchers replaced by one Mk 41 Mod 0 61-missile VLS for 45 BGM-109 Tomahawk SLCM and ASROC; Mk 16 octuple launchers for ASROC deleted.
Propulsion: Four GE LM-2500 gas-turbines (86,000shp); two shafts; 32.5kts.

By the 1960s the large number of Second World War-vintage destroyers serving in the US Navy were worn-out and in urgent need of replacement, and the Spruance class was designed to replace them. They are much larger ships, intended principally for ASW work. One of the aims was to build as many ships as possible with the money available; so, although they are large and very seaworthy ships, they have a relatively small number of weapons systems for their hull-size. One of the measures intended to keep costs down was the use of a Total Procurement Package, which involved placing the entire production responsibility with one company at one site, which led to muddle, causing delays and

Below: Large and roomy, but relatively lightly-armed for their size, the Spruances are undergoing a major updating programme.

Above: A Tactical Display System suite undergoes a "chokedown" inside one Spruance class ship's Combat Information Centre. The class excels in the realm of anti-submarine warfare operations.

cost-overruns. Thirty ships were ordered, but the US Congress later added to the confusuion by insisting on an order for a 31st to an "air-capable" design, with an enlarged hangar for four helicopters. The ship, USS *Hayler* (DD 997), was completed, but as a virtually standard Spruance class design.

The success of the basic design is shown by the fact that both the Kidd class destroyers and the Ticonderoga class cruisers use virtually the same hull, which was designed to provide minimum rolling and pitching without the use of stabilizers. All three classes also use the same propulsion system, which is provided by four General Electric LM-2500 gas-turbines, which, at the time of its appearance, was the first such installation in a major US warship. It is controlled by just one operator at a central station and has proved both efficient and very quiet in service, being able to accelerate the ship from 12 to 32kts in just 53 seconds. The gas-turbines are paired, with two coupled through reduction gearing to each shaft, and cruising range can be greatly extended by closing-down one engine on each shaft.

Naturally, the armament and sensors installed in these ships have undergone change and development since they entered service, one indication being that the crew has increased from 232 enlisted men to the present 315, an increase of 36 per cent! In addition, individual ships have often been used for "one-off" tests of new systems. As a result, at any one time there are marked variations in the weapons across the class.

In 1974 the then Shah of Iran placed an order for six developments of the Spruance class, which were to be the core of his rapidly expanding navy. The order was later reduced to four, but after Ayatollah Khomeini took over the order was cancelled. Fortunately, Congress authorized completion of these ships for the US Navy and they joined the fleet in 1981/82 as the Kidd (DDG 993) class at the "bargain" price of $510 million each. They use the Spruance hull, but are optimized for the air defence role, with two Mk 29 launchers for Standard SM-1 MR SAMs and an SPS-48E 3-D radar. They are very well fitted-out and as their air-conditioning was designed for service with the Iranian Navy have proved very effective for Gulf deployments under the US flag!

Nuclear-Powered Attack Submarines (SSN)

Some twenty years ago it was being confidently predicted that nuclear-powered submarines would take over from conventionally-powered vessels in all but the smallest navies. This has not happened, mainly because of the expense and resources (especially technical manpower) required for the SSNs, and, as shown later in the book, there are still many hundreds of SSKs in service.

The SSN combines in its hull considerable carrying capacity with endurance. The carrying capacity is devoted to weapons and sensors, while the endurance frees the submarines from that most vulnerable of all activities, approaching the surface — except when the need arises to communicate with base.

The key element in an SSN's sensors is the sonar, and in their submarines US designers have devised large sonar arrays which take up the entire bow. This has meant that the torpedo tubes have had to be moved further back on the hull and are now angled outwards at some 10°, although this approach has not been followed by other SSN-equipped navies. One of the problems facing SSNs is that their sensors outperform their weapons, especially the torpedo, which is a slow-travelling device and reasonably easy to detect. Thus both the Russian and US Navies have introduced

submarine-launched missiles which travel for most of their journey through the air, delivering their payload in the vicinity of the target and ideally giving insufficient time for evasive action.

The Russian Akula class is a very significant design: made of titanium, and coated with anechoic tiles, the boats can travel at over 35kt, posing a major problem to surface ASW forces (which cannot move at anything like that speed) and outperforming most torpedoes in service. The US Los Angeles class is not as fast as the Akula but represents probably the most sophisticated warship system ever to enter service. The French Navy's Amethyste design is of interest in that it is considerably smaller than any other SSN, and the French are claiming that they have found different answers to the problems of size and noise in submarine nuclear propulsion systems from those employed by the Americans, although few details of the system have yet been made public.

Below: USS *Batfish*, the thirtieth of thirty-five nuclear-powered Sturgeon class attack submarines commissioned by the US Navy from 1967 to 1975. Despite their age, these boats pack a considerable punch in the form of Tomahawk and Harpoon missiles.

Akula Class

SSN (CIS)
Six boats + ? building.

Displacement: 7,500 tons surfaced; 9,100 tons submerged.
Dimensions: Length 377.3ft (115m); beam 45.9ft (14m); draught 34.1ft (10.4m).
Propulsion: Nuclear; 1 shaft; 32kt.
Armament: 6 25.6in (650mm) and/or 21in (533mm) torpedo tubes; tube-launched
SS-N-15, -16, -16B and -21 missiles; torpedoes.
Complement: 90 approx.

Whereas no Western navy — not even that of the USA — has produced more
than one class of SSN at a time, the navy of the former Soviet Union managed
to find the resources to produce two types simultaneously in the 1980s. One
was the Sierra class (qv), the other the larger Akula. They are the largest SSNs
ever built, being some 7.4ft (2.27m) longer than the US Navy's Los Angeles
class SSNs and with approximately 2,000 tons greater displacement. The class

has been built at a very slow rate; the first was launched in 1984, followed by one a year between 1986 and 1989. This suggests that they are complicated and therefore very expensive submarines, and it must be questionable whether construction can continue in the new circumstances following the break-up of the Soviet Union and the resulting defence cuts.

For many years NATO allocated alphabetical names to Soviet submarines, but when this class appeared in the Alliance had run through the complete alphabet for reporting names. They therefore allocated the Russia name *Akula* meaning 'shark'.

The hull shape is probably the most streamlined of any modern submarine and visually appears to be a development of the Alfa class, although in this case the hull is constructed of steel rather than titanium. The fin is faired into the hull as in the Alfa and suggests that the overall shape may well be an outcome of the large naval research programme into fish streamlining. A large pod is mounted on the vertical rudder, which houses a towed sonar array.

The actual type of missile/torpedo tubes fitted has not yet been determined. They may all be the usual 21in (533mm) tubes or, alternatively, may be a mix of these and the new 25.6in (650mm) tubes, which have been under development for some years.

The role for which these submarines were built was to defence Soviet Navy SSBNs in the so-called "bastions" in the Barents Sea and the Sea of Okhotsk. There they would have sought to intercept Western SSBNs before they could get near enough to launch a pre emptive attack.

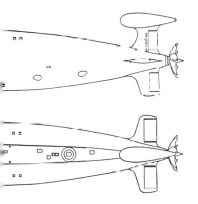

Left: One of the most visible distinguishing features of the Akula class is the long, low sail, quite unlike anything found on the West's SSNs. The large "teardrop" atop the rudder is a housing for a towed sonar array.

Below: An Akula class submarine caught on the surface by a US Navy maritime patrol aircraft, and recorded on film to add to the intelligence file held on this design. Nuclear-powered, these boats have a top speed of 32kt when dived.

Alfa Class

SSN (CIS)
Five boats

Displacement: 2,900 tons surfaced; 3,680 tons submerged.
Dimensions: Length 267.0ft (81.4m); beam 31.2ft (9.5m); draught 23.0ft (7.0m).
Propulsion: Nuclear, 47,000shp 1 shaft; 45kt submerged.
Armament: 6 21in (533mm) torpedo tubes; tube-launched SS-N-15 missiles;
Type 53 torpedoes; mines (in lieu of torpedoes).
Complement: 45.

The first Alfa class SSN was completed in the Sudomekh Yard in Leningrad
in 1972, but after two years of testing was broken-up in 1974, reportedly as
a result of a major leak from the nuclear reactor. Despite this the type entered
production and five joined the Soviet fleet between 1979 and 1983.

The Alfa class submarines are much shorter than any other SSN produced
for the erstwhile Soviet Navy, and are powered by two very small nuclear reactors,
which use liquid-metal (a lead-bismuth mixture) as a coolant. The engine room
and controls are highly-automated. They are, nevertheless, very powerful and
the boats are extremely fast, having been reported to have run under NATO
task forces at speeds of up to 40kt.

The hull is constructed of titanium alloy, and the lengthy construction time
is almost certainly mainly due to the difficulty of fabricating this material. It is,
however, very strong and enables the Alfa class boats to dive to depths of some
3,000ft (914m), far deeper than any other known submarine. The long, low sail
and the total absence of any protruding devices indicate that considerable
attention has been paid to reducing the noise signature.

There is a large low frequency (LF) sonar in the bows and each boat is fitted
with six 21in (533mm) torpedo tubes for conventional torpedoes and SS-N-15
missiles. When it appeared, the Alfa class was at the very forefront of submarine
technology and was treated with great respect by NATO navies. A major concern
at the time was that the Alfa's top speed was equal to the speed of NATO
torpedoes, which gave ASW commanders a major problem. This did, in fact,
spur NATO to develop much faster torpedoes which began to enter service
in the late 1980s.

Below: Alfas are made of titanium and coated with Clusterguard.

Sierra Class

SSN (CIS)

Three boats + ? building

Displacement: 6,050 tons surfaced; 8,200 tons submerged.
Dimensions: Length 361.03ft (110.0m); beam 41.0ft (12.5m); draught 24.3ft (7.4m).
Propulsion: Nuclear, 45,000shp; 1 shaft; 35kt submerged (approx).
Armament: 4 25.6in (650mm), 4 21in (533mm) torpedo tubes; tube-launched SS-N-15, -16 and -21 missiles; Type 53 and Type 65 torpedoes.
Complement: 70 (approx).

Following the Alfa and Victor classes (qqv), no less three new types of Soviet nuclear-propelled attack submarines appeared in the early 1980s. One was the single Mike class boat, displacing 5,700 tons submerged, which was officially described as being intended to test 12 new technologies, two of which were exotic materials (the hull was constructed of titanium) and "deep-sea problems". Despite its experimental status the Mike appears to have been built as a fully operational boat, with a torpedo armament and the normal range of sensors. Unfortunately, the Mike was lost in the Barents Sea on 7 April 1989 with the loss of 42 out of 67 members of her crew, and subsequent Soviet news releases revealed that of her load of twelve torpedoes, two had nuclear warheads. No further Mike class submarines have been built.

The other two types did, however, enter production. One was the Akula class (qv), the other the Sierra class. The first Sierra was launched in July 1983 at the inland shipyard at Gorkiy and was then moved via canal and river to be fitted out at Severodvinsk. Externally, there are similarities with the Victor III class, with a flattened top to the hull, a short sail which is not faired into the deck, a similar arrangement of free-flood holes and a large pod on top of the rudder.

Sierra class boats have been built at a very slow rate, the second being launched in 1986 and the third in 1989. It would appear that, following Soviet practice in the aircraft world, it was decided to develop the Akula and Sierra classes simultaneously, with each being an insurance against the failure of the other. It would appear, however, that, if this is the case, it is the Akula which has won the competition as no new Sierra class boat has been built since 1989, whereas the Akula remains in low-rate production.

Below: A Sierra I with the large pod atop the rudder revealed.

Victor I-III Class

SSM (CIS)

Victor-I — sixteen boats; **Victor-II** — seven boats.
Victor-III — twenty-four boats.

Displacement: 4,900 tons surfaced; 6,000 tons submerged.
Dimensions: Length 347.8ft (106.0m); beam 32.8ft (10.0m); draught 23.0ft (7.0m).
Propulsion: 2 pressurized-water nuclear-reactors; steam turbines; 1 shaft; 30,000shp; 29kt submerged.
Armament: 4 25.6in (650mm), 2 21in (533mm) torpedo tubes; tube-launched SS-N-15/-16/-21 missiles; Type 53 torpedoes; mines (in lieu of torpedoes).
Complement: 85.
(*Specifications above apply to Victor-III*).

First seen by Western observers in 1968, the Victor class is a second-generation Soviet nuclear-powered attack submarine. Somewhat shorter than the November class, but with as great a beam, sixteen of the first type — Victor-I — were built. These were followed by the Victor-II, which is 15ft 3in (4.6m) longer to enable it to carry the SS-N-15 missile. Only seven of these boats were built before production changed to yet another development, 11ft 6in (3.5m) longer

still and with a cylindrical pod mounted on top of the upper rudder. This has subsequently been confirmed as the first Soviet towed sonar array, and this interesting device has subsequently appeared on all-new Soviet/Russian attack submarines. Other sensors are a large, low-frequency sonar array in the bow, and a medium-frequency array for torpedo control. It is also reported that Victor-III hulls are coated with the Clusterguard anechoic protection to attenuate the reflections which are returned to searching hostile warships. There are now twenty-four Victor-IIIs, production having continued until it was certain that the Sierra and Akula classes would be a success.

On 27 February 1982, the Italian Sauro class submarine *Leonardo da Vinci* detected a Victor-I at a depth of some 984ft (300m), twenty-five miles (40km) south-east of the naval base at Taranto. The Italians tracked the Soviet submarine for some eighteen hours until it left Italian territorial waters. In reporting this incident the Italian authorities made it clear that this was by no means the first such incursion by a Soviet submarine. It is also noteworthy that the public announcement was absolutely positive about the nationality *and type* of the target, a rare acknowledgement of the precision of modern underwater identification technology.

Below: Running on the surface, this Victor-III displays the large fin-top pod containing a towed-array sonar unit. The hull is coated with Clusterguard anechoic tiling to reduce acoustic signature.

Rubis & Amethyste Classes

SSN (France)
Four boats + four building/four building

Displacement: 2,670 tons submerged.
Dimensions: Length 241.53ft (73.6m); beam 24.95ft (7.6m); draught 21.0ft (6.4m).
Propulsion: Nuclear 48MW; 1 shaft; 28kt.
Armament: 4 21in (533mm) torpedo tubes; tube-launched SM 39 Exocet missiles; F17 Mod 2 and L5 Mod 3 torpedoes; FG 29 mines.
Complement: 65.

France came late on to the nuclear submarine scene and, under strong pressure from President de Gaulle, went straight to SSBNs. Such a massive programme, which for political reasons had to be entirely French in character, took up all the available national resources for many years. It was not until the 1974 naval

programme, therefore, that the French Navy was able to turn its attention to SSNs, with the first of the SNA72 class — *Rubis* — being laid down in December 1976 and launched on 7 July 1979. She joined the fleet in 1982, following extensive trials. She was joined by three more boats over the years 1984-88 and two squadrons were formed, one based at Brest the other at Toulon.

The four Rubis class boats were followed by four improved versions of the Améthyste class, this being both the name of the first-of-class and an acronym for *Amélioration Tactique Transmission Écoute* (Reduced Radiated Transmission Drive). These eight boats are the smallest operational SSNs in any navy, which has been made possible by the radically new design of the nuclear propulsion system adopted.

Both Rubis and Améthyste class are fitted with four 21in (533mm) torpedo tubes, for which they carry F17 Mod 2 and L5 Mod 3 ASW torpedoes, SM 39 Exocet anti-ship missiles and FG 29 mines. The total warload is fourteen, the actual numbers of each carried depending upon the tactical mission.

The French Navy obtains greater productivity out of these SSNs by allocating two crews to each boat, which other navies only do with SSBNs. Whether they will continue to do so in the new and much reduced threat environment remains to be seen.

Left. A bird's-eye view of *Rubis*, her progress slowed almost to a halt to facilitate the extraction of a crewman by a French Navy Lynx helicopter. Operational since early 1983, *Rubis* underwent an extensive refit programme in 1986/88.

Below: Bedecked in her national colours, *Amethyste* takes to the water for the first time on 14 May 1988, Her name is an acronym for *AMElioration Tactique HYdrodynamique, Silence Transmission Ecoute* (Reduced Radiated Transmission Drive) and her design includes a new bow form as part of a major silencing programme.

Swiftsure Class

SSN (UK)
Six boats

Displacement: 4,400 tons surfaced; 4,900 tons submerged.
Dimensions: Length 272ft (82.9m); beam 32.25ft (9.83m); draught 27ft (8.2m).
Propulsion: 1 pressurized-water nuclear reactor; 2 steam turbines, 15,000shp; 1 shaft; 30kt dived.
Armament: 5 21in (533mm) torpedo tubes; Tigerfish Mk 24 Mod 2 torpedoes; UGM-84B Sub-Harpoon SSMs; mines (in lieu of torpedoes).
Complement: 97.

The Royal Navy first studied the possibility of nuclear propulsion for submarines in 1946 and a naval section started work at the atomic research station at Harwell in 1954. This national programme led to an operational system, although Britain's first nuclear submarine, HMS *Dreadnought*, launched in 1960, was actually powered by a US S5W reactor, which had been purchased from the United States.

The British reactor was installed in the second nuclear submarine, HMS *Valiant* (4,900 tons submerged displacement), which was completed in July 1966. Apart from the reactor and an increase in length she was generally similar to *Dreadnought*. Four more were built, the last joining the fleet in 1971. The Valiant class was scheduled to serve well into the 1990s, but the reduction in the size of the Royal Navy in the early 1990s has led to them being retired early, the last two to go being HMS' *Valiant* and *Courageous*.

The third class of British SSNs were the Swiftsures, the first of which joined the fleet in April 1973. These boats are 13ft (4m) longer than the Valiants, with a flat upper deck which maintains the maximum diameter for a much greater length and gives a completely different shape from the 'humped back' of earlier

British SSNs. This new shape is evidence of greater internal volume in the pressure hull, leading to more equipment space and better living conditions. The fin is not as tall as on the earlier classes, and the diving planes are set much lower and further forward (and are not, in fact, visible when the boat is on the surface). There are five torpedo tubes with twenty reloads, a heavy armament for the size of the hull. The torpedoes are the latest Tigerfish Mk 24 (Modified), and reload time is reported to be fifteen seconds per tube.

These submarines are exceptionally quiet, having been built with rafted engines and shrouded propellers. During refits they have also had their hulls and sails coated with anechoic tiles to reduce their sonar signatures yet further. All underwent further long refits in the mid/late 1980s and are now scheduled to serve on well into the 21st Century.

The three Valiant class boats and two of the Swiftsure class took part in the 1982 Falklands War. A Valiant class submarine, HMS *Conqueror*, became the only nuclear submarine in any navy to have sunk a hostile warship when she torpedoed the Argentine cruiser ARA *General Belgrano* on 2 May 1982. *Belgrano*, in company with two destroyers, was on a sweep to the south of the Falkland Islands when she was intercepted and the British SSN fired two torpedoes (actually World War Two-vintage Mark 8s!), both of which hit. The cruiser sank with considerable loss of life and the two destroyers carried out a series of depth-charge attacks on the SSN before returning to rescue survivors. All five SSNs were then responsible for the blockade which effectively kept the Argentine Navy in port for the remainder of the war. The whole episode demonstrated the offensive capability of the SSNs and showed how helpless a navy with limited ASW capability is against such a sophisticated threat.

Below: HMS *Splendid* (S 106), sixth and final boat in the Swiftsure class, serves with the 3rd Submarine Squadron, Royal Navy. During the 1990s, Spearfish torpedoes will be added as primary armament.

Trafalgar Class

Fleet submarines
Seven boats (S 87-S 88, S 90-S 93, S 107).

Country of origin: United Kingdom.
Displacement: 4,700 tons surfaced (5,208 tons submerged).
Dimensions: Length overall 280.1ft (85.4m); beam 32.1ft (9.8m); depth 31.2ft (9.5m).
Armament: Five 21in (533mm) tubes for Tigerfish Mk 24 Mod 2 and Spearfish torpedoes; UGM-84B Sub-Harpoon SSM; ground mines.
Propulsion: One pressurized water-cooled PWR nuclear reactor (4,000hp); one shaft; pump jet propulsion (except **S 107**); 32kts submerged.

The seven boats of the Trafalgar class closely follow the design of the previous Swiftsures, which proved a great success. This latter class had shorter, fatter hulls coupled with a shorter sail which reduced the periscope depth. They also had a coating of the new anechoic tiles for noise reduction which made them

Below: Assigned to the 2nd Submarine Squadron, Royal Navy, HMS *Tireless* (S 88) is one of seven Trafalgar class boats ordered.

Above: A complement of 97 crew, 12 of whom are officers, man each Trafalgar class boat. Additional boats may yet be built.

Overleaf: HMS _Turbulent_ (S 87), seen here surfacing, was the first-of-class boat. Additional boats may yet be built.

the quietest of SSNs. As six years had passed between the two designs it was possible to incorporate the many advances made in detection and electronics, and the Trafalgars incorporate the latest in "quietening" technology. Other improvements include a propulsion plant featuring a new core which has a longer life than previous types.

The increased size of the Trafalgar class boats and the many improvements made to their equipment has greatly increased their individual cost. Back in 1976, HMS _Swiftsure_ (the first of her class) cost £37.1 million; the cost for the fifth boat in the class — HMS _Spartan_ — rose to £68.9 million. Costs are even higher within the Trafalgar class. HMS _Torbay_ (the fourth boat) has now cost £176 million; whilst HMS _Triumph_ has cost over £200 million!

In order to achieve even quieter running, the machinery raft is suspended from bulkheads at each end of the engine spaces and not the hull as in the Swiftsure class. A pump jet is employed instead of the conventional propeller, so cutting down even more on noise. Such improvements occasionally present problems (and here it is weight), but the additional buoyancy of the tail cone enables this extra load to be carried. Trials with the pump jet were not completed in time for the system to be used in the first-of-class, HMS _Trafalgar_, and a conventional shaft was fitted; but the pump has been incorporated in subsequent boats. The hulls are covered in anechoic tiles to further reduce the acoustic sound level. These boats also carry a new array of sensors, with the Type 2020 sonar in the bow and a Type 2019 mounted ahead of the fin. Torpedo tubes are fitted as in the Swiftsure boats, with two firing from each side, the four tubes being angled out from abaft the bow sonar. The fifth tube is located on the underside of the hull. Both Tigerfish and Spearfish torpedoes are carried. The Tigerfish wire-guided/acoustic-homing ASW torpedo has an electric motor with twin contra-rotating propellers; speed is approximately 50kts and range is 11nm (21km). Spearfish is also wire-guided, with active/passive homing to 34nm (65km) at 60kts. Also carried is the Sub-Harpoon SSM, a sub-launched version of the US anti-ship missile which has proved highly successful. Urchin and Stonefish ground mines can be carried in place of torpedoes.

HMS _Trafalgar_ was ordered in 1977, laid down in 1979 and commissioned in 1983. Five more units (HMS' _Turbulent, Tireless, Torbay Trenchant_ and _Talent_) followed from 1984 to 1990, leavng the final boat (HMS _Triumph_) to be completed during 1992. Looking to the future, plans to modernize the fleet will include trials with a revised wet end to the towed sonar, and an upgraded radar.

Los Angeles/Lipscomb Classes

SSN (USA)

Thirty + 20 building + 7 ordered/one boat

Displacement: 6,900 tons submerged.
Dimensions: Length 360ft (109·7m); beam 33ft (10·1m); draught 32·3ft (9·8m).
Propulsion: Nuclear, 35,000shp; 1 shaft; 30+kt dived.
Armament: Harpoon and Tomahawk missiles; SUBROC; 4 21in (533mm) torpedo tubes.
Complement: 127.
(Specifications given for Los Angeles class.)

Lipscomb was launched in 1973, the outcome of a development programme for a 'quiet' submarine stretching back to the *Tullibee* (qv) of the early 1960s. *Lipscomb* has many interesting features to achieve silent running, many of which have subsequently been incorporated into the Los Angeles class, although the turbo-electric plant, which removes the requirement for gearing (the prime source of noise in SSNs), was not. *Lipscomb* is still in front-line service.

The first Los Angeles class SSN entered service in 1976; thirty are now in commission, twenty are under construction and a further seven are on order, making this one of the most massive and expensive defence programmes undertaken by any nation. The Los Angeles boats are much larger than any previous US Navy SSN and have a higher submerged speed. They have the very long-range BQQ-5 sonar and the BQS-15 short-range system, and also operate towed arrays. Weapons fits can include SUBROC, Harpoon and Tomahawk, as well as conventional and wire-guided torpedoes. Thus, like all other US SSNs, although they are primarily intended to hunt and destroy other submarines and to protect SSBNs, the Los Angeles submarines can also be used without modification to sink surface ships at long range, while Tomahawk will enable them to attack strategic targets well inland. The BQQ-5 sonar is particularly effective, and is reported on one occasion to have enabled an American SSN to track two Soviet Victor class (qv) SSNs simultaneously.

The Los Angeles class is very sophisticated and each boat is an extremely potent fighting machine; moreover, with a production run of at least 57 boats it must be considered a very successful design. Nevertheless, the class is also becoming very expensive: in 1976 the cost of each boat was estimated at $221·25 million, but the boat bought in FY79 cost $325·6 million and the two in FY81 $495·8 million each. Not even the USA can continue to spend money at that rate.

Below: The launch of a Los Angeles class SSN illustrates the size of these vessels. These are the most effective of all nuclear-powered attack submarines, with ASW sensors and weapons, anti-ship missiles and strategic cruise missiles, enabling them to carry out a variety of important naval functions.

Below: USS *Atlanta* (SSN-712). At least 57 of these boats are to be built, with current costs running at $US495·8 million per unit, making this possibly the most expensive defence programme ever. The Los Angeles class is designed to protect US carrier groups and attack Soviet SSBNs, both vital tasks.

Sturgeon/Narwhal Classes

SSN (USA)

Thirty-five/one boat

Displacement: SSN-637 to SSN-677 — 4,250 tons surfaced; 4,780 tons submerged. **SSN-678 to SSN-687 plus modernized units** — 4,460 tons surfaced, 4,960 tons submerged.

Dimensions: SSN-637 to SSN-677 — length 360.0ft (109.73m), **SSN-678 to SSN-687 and modernized units** — 302.2ft (92.1m); **all** — beam 33.0ft (10.06m); **all** — draught 32.0ft (9.75m).

Propulsion: 1 Westinghouse S5W2 pressurized-water nuclear-reactor; steam turbines; 1 shaft; 20,000shp; 30kt submerged.

Armament: 4 21in (533mm) torpedo tubes; 15 Mk 48 torpedoes; 4 Sub-Harpoon and 4 Subroc SSM; up to 8 Tomahawk SLCM/SSM in place of other weapons.

Complement: 107.

(Specifications are for Sturgeon class).

The 35 Sturgeon class SSNs are slightly larger and improved versions of the Permit design. They have an Albacore-type hull with the four torpedo tubes amidships to clear the bow for the BQQ-2 sonar system, and can be distinguished from the earlier class by the taller sail with diving planes set lower down to facilitate control at periscope depth; these diving planes can be rotated to the vertical when surfacing through ice. There were several problems during the building of this class: one boat had to be moved to another yard to be completed, while another sank in 35ft (10.7m) of water while fitting out.

Although American SSNs are already very quiet, anything which can be done to reduce the noise signature is speedily introduced and tested by the US Navy. An experimental SSN, essentially a lengthened Sturgeon class boat, is *Narwhal*, built to test the S5G free-circulation reactor, which has no pumps and is, therefore, quieter than previous US reactors. However, whilst *Narwhal* retains this system and is still in service, no further submarines have been built with such a system.

The last nine boats of the Sturgeon class were built 10ft (3m) longer to accommodate additional sonar and electronic gear and nineteen of the earlier boats have had their BQQ-2 sonar replaced by the BQQ-5 equipment in the course of routine refits.

Left: USS *Bergal* (SSN-667): a dramatic shot of an emergency surfacing drill, which allows a rare glimpse of the bow profile of a US SSN. By positioning the torpedo tubes amidships the designers have been able to put a massive sonar array in the bow.

Below: USS *Tunny* (SSN-682) under way in the Atlantic, showing the great length of these US SSNs, which, combined with their large diameter, gives vast internal volume. All the Sturgeon class have had their BQQ-2 sonar replaced by the BQQ-5 to upgrade the boats to Los Angeles class standard.

Conventional Submarines (SSK)

Some years ago it was forecast that all future submarines in the major navies would be nuclear-powered. However, things have turned out somewhat differently, and diesel-electric submarines are found in almost every fleet, only the US Navy having attained a virtual all-nuclear status (although the French have also committed themselves to such a goal). The former Soviet Navy retains about one hundred conventional boats in service and is producing more every year. The modern conventional submarine has advantages to offer, not least economy. The four Los Angeles class SSNs constructed in FY87 cost $656.3 million each; these are sophisticated, deep-ocean boats, but few navies can afford costs of that order. SSNs also require large crews (Los Angeles: 127, Swiftsure: 97) compared to diesel-electric boats (Type 209: 33, Upholder: 46).

Nuclear submarines are very powerful and fast (over 40kt in some cases), and their endurance is only really limited by crew fatigue. SSNs cannot, however avoid making some noise, which renders them liable to detection, particularly within the confines of the continental shelf. Conventional boats are much quieter when running on their electric motors, and therefore more suitable for ASW patrol, reconnaissance and clandestine missions. Excellent examples of the last were afforded by the Soviet Whiskey class boat which ran aground in Swedish territorial waters in late 1981, and by the UK's HMS *Opossum,* which transported special forces in the Gulf area during the 1991 Gulf War.

Conventional submarine development is now at a critical stage, with many existing types becoming due for replacement and several navies wanting to operate submarines for the first time. There are several types in production of which the German and Swedish have been the most successful so far. The British Upholder class is undoubtedly the most sophisticated of these designs and is the most combat-effective and versatile, but it has also proved far too expensive for other navies. For once, the USA has totally opted out of this field and finds itself with nothing to offer.

Modern conventional submarines fall into three categories. The first is the 400-600-ton coastal boat such as the German Type 205/206 and the Italian Toti class. These are effective in their way, but suffer from limitations in range, torpedo reloads and sensor capacity. The next size is the 900-1,300-ton group, for example the German Type 209, the Yugoslavian Sava and the Swedish Näcken and Sjöormen classes. These, too, are limited in endurance and carrying capacity and are to be found in the smaller navies with medium-range roles.

Right: The majority of today's conventional submarines fall into the 1,600+ ton category, an example being the three Walrus class boats operated by the Netherlands Navy, of which the lead boat is shown here. Twenty torpedoes or missiles can be carried.

Kilo Class

SSK (CIS)
Twenty-four boats (more building)

Displacement: 2,400 tons surfaced; 2,800 tons submerged.
Dimensions: Length 239.5ft (73.0m); beam 32.5ft (9.90m); draught 21.3ft (6.5m).
Propulsion: 3 diesel generator sets; 1 electric motor, 6,800shp; 1 shaft; 20kt.
Armament: 6 21in (533mm) torpedo tubes; Type 53 torpedoes; mines (in ieu of torpedoes).
Complement: 53.

The Tango class (qv) has a long, narrow hull, of a type which has been found to have limits in speed and manoeuvrability, and which has been discontinued in other navies in favour of the shorter, fatter "Albacore" hull. The latest Russian diesel-electric submarine, however — the Kilo class — does sport this new type of hull. The Kilo was first seen in the Far East in 1981 and has since been produced at two yards: Komsomolsk-na-Amur in the Far East and Gorki in European Russia.

The hull of the Kilo is some 65ft (20m) shorter than that of the Tango but with a somewhat broader beam. The result is a submarine with many similarities to the US Barbel and the Dutch Zwaardvis. There are, however, a number of difference which mark the Kilo as being a Russian design. The most evident of these is the line of free-flood holes along the outer casing, which testifies to Russian persistence with double-hull construction. The second characteristic feature is the long sail. The third is the position of the retractable, forward hydroplanes, which are located just beneath the deck casing and immediately forward of the sail.

The Kilo class is also the first Russian diesel-electric class to have just one shaft and a single six-bladed propeller. All previous SSKs have had at least two shafts and some, such as the Tango, had three.

Unlike the Tango class, the Kilo class has been sold for export. Customers so far have included Algeria (two), India (eight), Poland (one) and Romania (one). It is believed that Cuba, Iran and Libya have also placed orders.

Below: A small number of Kilo class boats have been exported over the years, including this example supplied to the Polish Navy. Too big for Baltic operations, it remains the only example acquired.

Tango Class

SSK (CIS)
Eighteen boats

Displacement: 3,100 tons surfaced; 3,900 tons submerged.
Dimensions: Length 301.8ft (92m); beam 29.5ft (9m); draught 23ft (7m).
Propulsion: 3 diesel, 6,000bhp; 3 electric, 6,000shp; 3 shafts; 16kt dived.
Armament: 10 21in (533mm) torpedo tubes.
Complement: 62.

The CIS Navy has a vast fleet of conventional submarines: at least 100 are currently in service, with more in reserve. A few Whiskey-V remain in service, and it was one of these that ran aground near the Swedish naval base at Karlskrona in 1982. The next class was the Romeo, an improved Whiskey, of which 56 were initially planned although this was cut back to twenty when the nuclear fleet was expanded. Some of the Foxtrot class also remain in service, built between 1958 and 1971 for the erstwhile Soviet Navy.

The Tango class was first seen by Western observers at the Sebastopol Naval Review in July 1973, and production continued at a rate of some two to three boats per year until 1982. This class is of advanced design, and it is of interest that the Soviet Union did not seem particularly keen to export it, despite the considerable market for a conventionally-powered submarine of this size and capability. It is clearly regarded as complementary to the SSNs, and could well be intended for use in the extensive shallow waters around the CIS.

The hull of the Tango class has very smooth lines, but one noteworthy feature is that forward of the fin there is a marked rise of some 3ft (0.91m). This will undoubtedly improve seakeeping qualities on the surface, but also suggests a requirement for extra volume in the forward end of the boat, possibly for some new weapon system; it has also been reported that the latest boats have a slightly longer hull to allow for a new weapon to be fitted. The smooth lines of these submarines suggest a small and compact design, but this is deceptive as they are, in fact, the largest conventional submarines built since World War II.

Below: The unusual rise in the bow lines of the Tango class can be seen in this view, a feature thought to indicate the carriage of a new weapon system. Each boat has eight 21in (533mm) torpedo tubes.

Agosta Class

SSK (France)
Ten boats

Displacement: 1,490 tons surfaced; 1,740 tons submerged.
Dimensions: Length 221.7ft (67.6m); beam 22.3ft (6.8m); draught 17.7ft (5.4m).
Propulsion: 2 diesel, 3,600bhp; 1 electric, 4,600hp; 1 shaft; 20kt dived.
Armament: 4 21in (533mm) torpedo tubes.
Complement: 54.

Agosta, name ship of the class, joined the French fleet in July 1977 and was followed by three more in 1977-78, completing the French Navy's own order. A further four Agostas have been built in Spain by Bazan. The South Africans ordered two as well, but this was blocked for political reasons and they were sold to Pakistan, instead. Egypt was interested at one time in purchasing two Agostas, but no order has ever been announced.

Somewhat larger than the previous Daphnés, the Agosta class is intended for distant-water operation. Only four torpedo tubes are fitted, but there are twenty reloads and special devices for rapid reloading. The tubes are 21in (533mm) in diameter, the first time that the French have abandoned their previous 21.7in (550mm); this is presumably intended to enhance the export potential of the type. ASW equipment includes a passive sonar set (DSUV-2) with thirty-six microphones, two active sets, and a passive ranging set under a spiky dome on the foredeck. Great attention has been devoted to silent running, and an unusual feature is the fitting of a small 30hp electric motor for very quiet, low-speed movement whilst on patrol.

If the French Navy sticks to its announced intention to concentrate on nuclear-powered submarines in future, the Agosta class could be the last of a distinguished and interesting line of French conventional boats.

Above: An MCC 32C mine is loaded aboard one of the Agostas. Each of these weapons (36 of which can be carried in lieu of torpedoes) has a 1,168lb (530kg) TNT warhead. In addition to torpedoes and mines, the Agostas can carry and fire SM 39 Exocet SSMs.

Below: Originally home-ported at the Mediterranean port of Toulon, all four of the Agosta class boats now operate from the Atlantic port of Lorient. These diesel-powered SSKs were the first French Navy submarines to be fitted with 21in (533mm) torpedo tubes.

Type 206

SSK (Germany)
Eighteen boats

Displacement: 450 tons surfaced; 500 tons submerged.
Dimensions: Length 159.45ft (48.60m); beam 15.01ft (4.60m); draught 14.11ft (4.30m).
Propulsion: 2 MTU diesel generator sets; 1 electric motor, 2,300shp; 1 shaft; 17kt.
Armament: 8 21in (533mm) torpedo tubes; 24 mines in external container.
Complement: 22.

Germany has a special place in the history of the submarine, ending World War II with some outstanding designs which, fortunately for the Allies, failed to attain operational status in significant numbers. It was not until 1954 that Germany was allowed to construct the Type 205, a small coastal boat, twelve of which were built for use in the Baltic.

Having completed the Type 205s, design work started on a follow-on class of Type 206 450-ton boats, the main concern being with greater battery power to meet the demands of the ever-increasing numbers of electrical and electronic devices but without reducing submerged speed or endurance. Construction of the first boat (*U-13*) began in November 1969, and the eighteenth and last joined the Bundesmarine in September 1971. Made of special non-magnetic steel, these submarines have served the German Navy well and, so far as is known, have totally avoided the notorious corrosion problems that affected the earlier Type 205s. The opportunity was taken in this class to upgrade the active and passive sonars and the fire-control system, and wire-guided torpedoes were fitted for the first time in a German submarine design.

The British Vickers Shipbuilding Group constructed three submarines for Israel under licence from Ingenieurkontor Lübeck (IKL) but fitted with British weapons systems. Described variously as an adaptation of the Type 206 or as a smaller Type 209, the IKL 540 is optimised for operations in the warmer waters of the eastern Mediterranean.

An unusual feature of these boats is the external minebelt, a strap-on container, which enables them to carry twenty mines in addition to their full load of twenty torpedoes. Most other submarines discharge mines from their torpedo tubes and can thus only carry mines at the expense of torpedoes.

Twelve of these submarines have been modernized, which involved fitting a new fire control system to enable them to fire Seeal 3 DM2A3 torpedoes instead of the previous DM2A1. Known as the Type 206A, these boats also feature the DBQS-21D sonar, new periscopes, refitted propulsion system and improvements to crew living and working areas.

Below: One of twelve German Navy Type 206 boats to be upgraded to Type 206A standard. All twelve of the improved boats are assigned to a squadron home-based at Eckernforde.

Type TR-1700

SSK (Germany)

Two boats; two building; two projected

Displacement: 2,150 tons surfaced; 2,364 tons submerged.
Dimensions: Length 216.5ft (66.0m); beam 23.95ft (7.30m); draught 21.33ft (6.50m).
Propulsion: 4 MTU diesel generator sets; 1 electric motor, 8,970shp; 1 shaft; 25kt.
Armament: 6 21in (533mm) torpedo tubes; AEG SST-4 wire-guided torpedoes; mines.
Complement: 30.

The Argentine Navy has operated submarines for many years and in 1974 it took delivery of two German Type 209 submarines, which were named the *Salta* and *San Luis*. In the 1982 Falklands War these two small boats caused great anxiety to the Royal Navy task force, although *Salta* was in refit and did not take part in the war. Much effort was expended in searching for *San Luis*, which operated in the area of the task force and fired six torpedoes, although she scored no hits. Both are currently being refitted to enable them to serve through to at least 2000.

In 1977 the Argentine Navy ordered five TR-1400 submarines from the German firm of Thyssen-Nordseewerke, an order which was changed to the larger Type 1700 in February 1982. The TR-1700 is a large submarine, with a submerged displacement of 2,364 tons, making it only marginally smaller than the British Upholder class. It has a particularly well streamlined shape and high power, which enable it to reach a maximum submerged speed of 25kt, probably the highest speed of any diesel-electric submarine. Such a speed could not, of course, be sustained for long, but it is still a remarkable achievement.

The TR-1700 is a single-hull design, which is of uniform diameter throughout, apart from a short tapered section aft. Internally it is divided into three sections by two transverse bulkheads. The adoption of extensive automation means that a crew of just thirty men is needed.

There are six 21in (533mm) torpedo tubes for which 22 German-made SST-4 wire-guided torpedoes are carried. An autoload device enables the tubes to be reloaded in just fifty seconds. Ground mines and Mk 37 torpedoes can also be carried.

The first two boats were built in Germany: *Santa Cruz* was launched in 1982 and commissioned in 1984, followed by *San Juan* in 1985. Three more are being built in Argentina, of which the first, which was laid down in 1983, eventually reached the fleet in 1991. Progress on the other two was even slower. All five have been offered for sale, but there have been no takers so far.

Below: *Santa Cruz* (S 41) on shakedown in German waters prior to her delivery to the Argentinian Navy in 1984. To date, just two of the four boats planned have been commissioned into service.

Type 209

SSK (Germany)
Thirty-four boats (plus more building)

Displacement: 1,105 tons surfaced; 1,230 tons submerged.
Dimensions: Length 180.4ft (55.0m); beam 20.34ft (6.20m); draught 19.36ft (5.90m).
Propulsion: 4 diesel; 1 electric motor, 5,000shp; 1 shaft; 22kt.
Armament: 8 21in (533mm) bow torpedo tubes; Sub-Harpoon SSM; 4 AEG SST torpedoes.
Complement: 31.
(Specifications are for Greek Type 209. Other sub-types differ; see text.)

When the Allies raised the submarine tonnage limit to 1,000 tons the (then) West German designers were able to design a new and larger boat on the general lines of the Type 205. This was very sensibly aimed at the export market and some remarkable successes have been achieved. As of early 1992, the operators included: Argentina (two), Brazil (two, plus four building), Chile (two), Colombia (two), Ecuador (two), Greece (eight), India (two, plus two building), Peru (six), Turkey (six, plus more building) and Venezuela (two). Brazil, India and Turkey have set up their own yard facilities for the Type 209.

There are various different versions, the largest being those for the Indian Navy, which displace 1,860 tons submerged. The Indian boats also have a central bulkhead, dividing the hull into two watertight compartments. They are also fitted with the IKL-designed "rescue-sphere" which enables up to forty men to escape simultaneously from a stricken submarine.

The Type 209 is similar in shape and layout to the earlier Type 205, but has increased dimensions, greater battery capacity and a more powerful propulsion system. The hull is completely smooth, with retractable hydroplanes mounted in the bows, cruciform aft control surfaces and a single propeller. Careful hull design and powerful motors give a "burst" speed of 23kt. They are designed for patrols of up to fifty days and are armed with eight 21in (533mm) torpedo tubes, for which they carry up to sixteen torpedoes the actual number and type depending on the customer.

These boats represent one of the most successful contemporary submarine designs and it is clear that the German designers have made a very good assessment of the export market. The type continues to attract orders, with boats currently being built for Israel and South Korea.

Above: Export orders for the Type 209 have flourished. This boat, the S30, was sold to the Brazilian Navy. Named the *Tupi* it is the first in the Brazilian Tupi class. This was planned to comprise of five other Type 209s. Delays, however, have placed this original plan in doubt.

Left: Seen underway, the S117 *Amphitrite* was commissioned into the Greek Navy in 1979, and is the sixth in their Glavkos class of submarines. The Greeks use the 1100 and 1200 Types of the 209. An update programme was begun in 1989 to bring the first four boats in the class up to the standard of the German S 206A class.

Salvatore Pelosi (Improved Sauro) Class

SSK (Italy)
Two boats + two building

Displacement: 1,476 tons surfaced; 1,662 tons submerged.
Dimensions: Length 211.2ft (64.36m); beam 22.38ft (6.82m); draught 18.57ft (5.66m).
Propulsion: 3 diesel; 1 electric, 4,270shp; 1 shaft; 19kt.
Armament: 6 21in (533mm) bow torpedo tubes.
Complement: 50.

Italy did not start to construct submarines in the post-war period until 1965, when the first of the Enrico Toti class was laid down. Four of these small boats were built. They have a 563-ton submerged displacement and a crew of 26, and are armed with four 21in (533mm) bow torpedo tubes, for which a total of just six torpedoes are carried. They are now somewhat elderly and one was withdrawn in 1990; the others will presumably follow soon.

The second post-war group was the Nazario Sauro class., four of which were commissioned between 1980 and 1982. These are much larger boats, with a submerged displacement of 1,637 tons, and are more heavily armed, having

six torpedo tubes. They carry twelve Italian-designed Whitehead Type A-184 ASW torpedoes. All four boats are to be given a mid-life refit by 1995, which will involve replacement of the batteries and some machinery, and improvements to the living accommodation.

Two new boats, designated the Salvatore Pelosi class (but also known as the "Improved Sauro" class), were completed in 1988/89. These have had a 1.64ft (0.5m) plug inserted amidships to accommodate an additional watertight bulkhead. They are being followed by two more boats in 1993/94, which may be even longer. Like the Nazario Sauro class, the Salvatore Pelosi class is fitted with six 21in (533mm) torpedo tubes. The last two of the Nazario Sauro class, however, and all of the Salvatore Pelosi class have longer tubes, which enable them to launch the Sub-Harpoon SSM, although curiously the Italian Navy has yet to place an order for these missiles.

The Sauro/Pelosi classes are very conventional submarines, intended specifically for ASW operations in the Mediterranean Sea. The Nazario Pelosi class boats are constructed of US HY-80 steel, which gives them a test depth of 984ft (300m) and a collapse depth of 1,968ft (600m).

Below: Cutting through the surface waters of the Mediterranean Sea is *Salvatore Pelosi* **(S 522), name boat of a class set to bring the Italian Navy's submarine flotilla to a strength of ten during the mid-1990s. The second pair of boats will have a slightly longer hull, and endurance will likely be increased 45 days.**

Yuushio Class

SSK (Japan)
Ten boats

Displacement: 2,250 tons surfaced.
Dimensions: Length 249.3ft (76m); beam 32.5ft (9.9m); draught 24.6ft (7.5m).
Propulsion: 2 diesel, 4,200bhp; 1 electric, 7,200hp; 1 shaft; 20kt dived.
Armament: 6 21in (533mm) torpedo tubes; Type 89 torpedoes; Sub-Harpoon SSM (seven boats).
Complement: 80.

The Japanese Maritime Self-Defence Force (JMSDF) produced its first indigenous post-war submarine design in 1959, a second, improved class in 1961-62 and then the four-boat Asashio class in the late 1960s. All have long since been stricken from JMSDF service.

The next class — Uzushio — was based on a US Navy design, with an Albacore-type 'teardrop' hull for faster and quieter underwater performance. The hull is of very high quality steel to permit a diving depth of up to 650ft (220m). Seven were built of which five remain in service.

The latest Japanese submarines are those of the Yuushio class, an all-round improvement on the Uzushio class and capable of slightly higher speeds. Both the Uzushio and Yuushio submarines have their torpedo tubes mounted amidships, firing outwards at an angle of 10° to the hull, a feature they share with the US Navy's SSNs. This is done in order to free the entire bow area for a large sonar array. The Uzushio class have pressure hulls of high-tensile steel (NS-63), permitting a diving depth of some 1,970ft (600m). The Yuushios, however, use even more modern steel (NS-90), giving a claimed diving depth of some 3,280ft (1,000m). The first two Yuushios will be retrospectively fitted with Sub-Harpoon missiles, but the remaining boats of the class were fitted with these missiles prior to delivery. A noteworthy feature of these Japanese submarines

Below: Forerunner of the Yuushio class was the Uzushio class, seven of which were built between 1968/75. Illustrated is *Isoshio*, one of the five remaining boats and currently serving the JMSDF as an auxiliary training submarine.

Above: *Mochishio*, second of the Yuushio class boats to be completed. The lines of this class are exceptionally clean, giving outstanding underwater performance. Though they look like SSNs, the Yuushio class boats are conventional diesel-electrics.

is their large complement, much greater for the size of hull than comparable boats in other navies.

These Japanese submarines are very advanced, as would be expected from such a technologically capable nation, and would seem to be fully equivalent to SSNs in most features except that of underwater endurance. This may be encouraging the JMSDF to seek a solution to the problem of freeing the non-nuclear submarine from the necessity of having to come up to the surface to 'breathe' at regular intervals.

The role of these Japanese submarines in war would be to defend Japanese waters from incursions by foreign surface and underwater vessels. The latest class of SSK for the JMSDF is the Harushio class, based on the Yuushio class but with a slight growth in overall dimensions. Six boats are on order.

Zwaardvis Class

SSK (Netherlands)
Two boats

Displacement: 2,350 tons surfaced; 2,640 tons submerged.
Dimensions: Length 219.6ft (66.92m); beam 27.56ft (8.40m); draught 23.3ft (7.10m).
Propulsion: 3 diesel, 4,200shp; 1 electric motor, 5,100shp; one shaft; 20kt.
Armament: 6 21in (533mm) bow torpedo tubes.
Complement: 65.

The two boats of the Zwaardvis class (*Zwaardvis* and *Tijgerhaai*) are among the largest conventional submarines currently in service, matched only by the Soviet Tango and British Upholder classes. The design of the Zwaardvis class was based on that of the US Navy's last diesel-electric submarine design, the Barbel class, with a similar Albacore-type "teardrop" hull. The design was, however, considerably modified to accommodate Dutch equipment. The two hulls were laid down in 1967 and both were delivered in 1972.

The hull is very deep, making the interior relatively spacious, accommodating two deck levels. Three diesel generators power the propulsion motor for surface running and are mounted on a false deck, which is suspended by springs from the hull to reduce radiated noise levels. Two groups of batteries provide underwater power and a "burst" speed well in excess of 20kts has been reported. A single, five-bladed propeller is mounted abaft the cruciform control surfaces. These two submarines underwent major refits in the late 1980s. Much new equiment was fitted including the British Type 2026 towed, passive array.

In 1980 the Taiwanese Navy placed an order for two "improved" versions of the Zwaardvis class, which were delivered in 1987/88 despite objections from the Chinese government in Beijing. Designated the Ha Lung (Sea Dragon) class, these are highly-automated submarines and carry the unusually high total of 28 torpedoes (compared with 20 in the original Zwaardvis design. The Taiwanese Navy has tried on several occasions to order four more of these excellent submarines, but the Dutch government has been pressured into refusing to accept the order.

Above: The *Tijgerhaai* (S-807),
one of the two Zwaardvis
class conventional submarines
of the Royal Netherlands
Navy. The *Tijgerhaai* was
updated in 1988 with Thomson
Sintra Eledone sonar and the
Signaal fire control system.
Both *Tijgerhaai* and her sister
boat *Zwaardvis* (S-806) are
expected to serve at least
until the end of the 1990s.

Left: Like her sister boat,
in the Zwaardvis class, the
Tijgerhaai carries up to
twenty torpedoes, two of
which can be launched at once.
Types of torpedo include the
Mk 48 Honeywell Mod 4, and NT
37D. Both are wire guided and
has active and passive homing.
These weapons give
the class a striking range of
up to 31 miles (50km/27nm).

Västergötland (A 17) Class

Patrol submarines
Four boats.

Country of origin: Sweden.
Displacement: 1,070 tons surfaced (1,143 tons submerged).
Dimensions: Length overall 159.1ft (48.5m); beam 20ft (6.1m); depth 18.4ft (5.6m).
Armament: Six 21in (533mm) tubes, three 15.75in (400mm) tubes; 12 FFV Type 613 torpedoes, six FFV Type 431 torpedoes; 22 mines (fitted externally).
Propulsion: Two Hedemora diesels, one electric motor (1,800shp); one shaft; 11kts surfaced (20kts submerged).

Since World War 2, the Royal Swedish Navy has equipped itself with successive classes of small but very effective submarines built at the Royal Swedish Dockyard at Karlskrona and the Kockums yard at Malmo. The Draken class of 1961-62 were the last to have the traditional hull form, but with the *Sjoormen*, launched in 1967, the modern form was introduced with its short, fat, circular hull without a deck casing. This group of five boats was followed by the three Näcken class boats and the slightly improved Västergötland class, the latter being acquired to replace the outdated Drakens.

Design contracts for the Västergötland class were awarded to Kockums in April 1978, with work commencing in December 1981. Kockums built the midship section and completed final assembly whilst Karlskrona built the bow and stern sections. These boats are single-hulled with an X-type rudder/hydroplane configuration. The Swedish Navy were the first to introduce this form of horizontal and vertical planes and soon began to appreciate its qualities of fine control. Furthermore, it allowed "bottoming" without damage in the shallow Baltic waters. Like the previous designs much thought has gone into achieving economy of space and these compact submarines are ideally suited for service in the relatively small Baltic Sea.

Above: A complement of 21 submariners crew each of the four
Västergötland class boats commissioned by the Swedish Navy.

Below: *Hälsingland*, the second-of-class boat, photographed in the
Baltic Sea prior to submerging. Torpedoes and mines constitute the
boats' weapons, SSMs having been rejected.

Upholder Class

Patrol submarines
Four boats (S 40-S 43).

Country of origin: United Kingdom.
Displacement: 2,455 tons submerged.
Dimensions: Length overall 230.6ft (70.3m); beam 25ft (7.6m); depth 7.7ft (5.5m).
Armament: Six 21in (533mm) tubes for Tigerfish Mk 24 Mod 2 and Spearfish torpedoes; UGM-84B Sub-Harpoon SSM; ground mines.
Propulsion: Two Paxman diesels, one electric motor (5,400hp); one shaft; 12kts surfaced (20kts submerged).

By the end of the 1970s, the Royal Navy was in need of a new class of non-nuclear submarine, and in 1979 plans were formulated for the Type 2400, later known as Upholder. The previous diesel-powered class, completed in 1967, had proved successful in service and were much quieter than their nuclear-powered counterparts. Moreover, Vickers (Barrow) were the only remaining shipyard in the UK with nuclear building experience, and they were already committed to the Trident programme, so cutting down on construction capacity.

The first boat (HMS *Upholder*) was laid down at the Vickers Shipbuilding and Engineering Yard at Barrow-in-Furness in November 1983, launched in December 1986 and commissioned in June 1990. Three more boats (HMS' *Unseen, Ursula* and *Unicorn*) are being built by Cammell Laird of Birkenhead, but the last of these will not be completed until 1993. Four more boats were originally planned but cancelled as a cost-cutting exercise and as a way of reducing the Royal Navy's diesel-powered submarine fleet to four boats by 1995.

The hull is single-skinned and made of high-tensile steel, with a "teardrop" shape for maximum underwater efficiency. The hull form has an unusually high beam to length ratio, and the large diameter of the pressure hull enables a spacious two-deck layout to be incorporated. Two watertight bulkheads divide the pressure hull into three main watertight compartments, with an acoustic bulkhead separating the propulsion room aft of the engine room. The overall design is amongst the best available, and like most modern submarines is capable of diving to great depth; in this case over 650ft (200m).

By using high-tensile steel greater strength is given to the hull structure, so

Below: HMS *Upholder* (S 40) was commissioned into service on 9 June 1990. A crew of 47 is carried, of which seven are officers.

enabling an increase of up to 50 per cent in diving depth. A decade ago, the Soviets were still using steel for the majority of submarines; but several classes have since been built of titanium which has greatly increased their diving capability (now estimated to be 2,000ft to 3,000ft (607m to 914m). By using titanium, which is non-magnetic, the hull is virtually undetectable to airbourne MAD and complex sea-laid coils, but welding the hull sections presents great problems. In the early-1970s, the West Germans tried to overcome the detection of their small Type 205, 206 and 207 submarines which usually operated in the shallow Baltic waters by using non-magnetic steel, but without success as corrosion proved too serious a problem.

Main machinery comprises two Paxman Valenta 1600 RPA-200 SZ diesels: the first time these engines have been fitted to submarines. At present, the Upholders carry Marconi Tigerfish Mk 24 Mod 2 torpedoes, but the more sophisticated and faster Spearfish will eventually be available. Both systems can be used either against surface craft or submarines. Endurance is 49 days, and each boat can run at 3kts submerged for 90 hours.

Below: Immediately apparent in this view of HMS *Upholder* is the very high sail, and the prominent sonar dome located on the foredeck.

Fixed-Wing Aircraft

Aircraft have been used to hunt and attack submarines since World War I, but they really came into their own in World War II. During the latter war ASW aircraft were generally either purpose-built flying-boats (e.g. Catalina, Sunderland) or converted bombers (Liberator, Lancaster). Today, however, the main type is the large converted civil airliner (Orion, Nimrod, May) although the purpose-built Atlantic is a particularly successful ASW design and just three types of flying boat remain. Only one fixed-wing ASW carrier-borne aircraft — the Lockheed Viking — serves in significant numbers.

Fixed-wing ASW aircraft offer long range, extended time on station and a good payload, devoted to both weapons and sensors. Their principal sensor is the sonobuoy, and they sow 'fields' which they can deploy rapidly and then monitor for hours at a time. They also carry a magnetic anomaly detector (MAD), with the magnetometer on a boom. Weapons carried include torpedoes, depth charges and depth bombs.

Well over 500 Lockheed P-3 Orions are in service around the world, and the type is being updated regularly; no successor airframe is being discussed at the moment. The corresponding Soviet aircraft is the Il-38 May, which is similar in most respects to the Orion. The Atlantic has sold well in Europe and is clearly an effective machine; it is, however, one of the few twin-engined, land-based ASW aircraft, most of the others being four-engined. One that stands apart is the British Nimrod, which is turbojet (as opposed to turboprop) powered. The argument for this is that it enables the aircraft to reach the scene of its patrol more rapidly, although the fact that the Comet was the only British airframe available at the time obviously had something to do with its selection.

Below: With several hundred examples patrolling on behalf of a dozen air arms, the Lockheed P-3 Orion is by far the most important of today's fixed-wing ASW platforms.

Harbin Shuihong-5 (PS-5)

(People's Republic of China)

Type: Long-range ASW flying-boat amphibian (crew of 8).
Dimensions: Length 127.63ft (38.9m); span 118.1ft (36.0m); height 32.12ft (9.79m).
Weight: Maximum 99,206lb (45,000kg).
Engines: 4 3,150ehp Dongan WJ5A turboprops.
Performance: Maximum speed 300kts (555km/h); range with maximum fuel 2,563nm (4,750km); endurance (2 engines) 12-15 hours.
Payload: Depth bombs, mines, anti-ship missiles and torpedoes.

The existence of the Chinese Shuihong 5 came as a complete surprise to the West when it was first revealed in the mid-1980s. Flying boats were widely used in the ASW role in World War Two and some new types were designed and built in the 1950s. From the 1960s onwards, however, the only two air arms with modern flying boats were those of the (then) Soviet Union, which operated the Beriev Be-12 Mail, and Japan, with the Shin Meiwa PS-1 and US-1.

Despite its apparent modernity, however, the Shuihong 5 is actually a contemporary of the Shin Meiwa PS-1, the Chinese aircraft's development having been seriously hampered by the disturbances of the Cultural Revolution. The fact that this was China's first, large, flying-boat may also have had something to do with the delays. The design was finalised in 1970 and the first prototype was completed in 1973, although the first flight did not actually take place until April 1976. Four more Shuihong 5s were completed and were handed over to the People's Liberation Army-Naval Air Force (PLA-NAF) in September 1976.

The Shuihong 5 is a high-wing aircraft, powered by four 3,150ehp turboprops. The long, narrow fuselage is unpressurized and has a single step on the planing-bottom. There is a prominent "thimble" radome in the nose, behind which is a semicircle of observation windows. There are two large, fixed floats beneath the wings. The aircraft is an amphibian and has a retractable undercarriage, with the main units retracting into wells in the side of the hull.

The five-man flight crew comprises pilot, co-pilot, navigator, flight engineer and radio operator. The mission crew of three have a large cabin in the centre of the fuselage. Sensors include the nose-mounted Doppler search/surveillance radar and a Magnetic Anomaly Detector (MAD) in the tail. There are four underwing hardpoints for sea-skimming missiles and lightweight torpedoes, and a weapons compartment in the rear of the fuselage houses more torpedoes, sonobuoys, mines or search-and-rescue gear.

Below: The production of the Shuihong 5 ended after five aircraft.

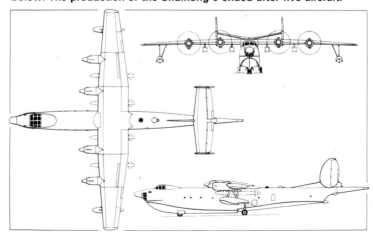

Beriev Be-12 (M-12) Mail

(Soviet Union)

Type: Multi-role reconnaissance amphibian (crew of 4-9).
Dimensions: Length 99ft (30·17m); span 97·5ft (29·71m); height 23ft (7m).
Weight: Empty 44,092lb (20,000kg); maximum 64,925lb (29,450kg).
Engines: Two 4,190ehp Ivchenko AI-20D single-shaft turboprops.
Performance: Maximum speed 329kt (610km/h); service ceiling 37,000ft (11,280m); range 2,160nm (4,000km); operational radius 702nm (1,300km).
Payload: Internal weapons bay for variety of ASW weapons; 2-4 underwing hardpoints for homing torpedoes or other stores.

Only two types of the once numerous ASW amphibians remain in service—the Soviet Beriev Be-12 and the Japanese Shin Meiwa PS-1—and even these are now gradually being phased out. The Beriev design bureau has produced a series of amphibious aircraft for the Soviet Naval Air Force over the years, but the M-12 Tchaika will almost certainly prove to have been the last of the line. Total production was of the order of 100 aircraft, all of which served with either the Black Sea or the Northern Fleet. None have been exported, and some seen over the Mediterranean in the 1960s in Egyptian markings were later discovered to have been Soviet Navy aircraft on detachment. Some eighty remain in service but, with the land-based Ilyushin Il-38 taking over the ASW role, most Be-12s have probably been relegated to second-line duties. Some ASW versions may, however, remain in service, perhaps with updated systems, for use in tactical situations where the ability to alight on water and conduct a sonar search may be of value.

The weapons bay is situated in the rear section of the fuselage, and there are two stores pylons under each wing; hatches in the rear fuselage permit weapons to be loaded while the aircraft is moored afloat. At least 6,500lb (3,000kg) of stores can be carried, and during a record-breaking flight in 1974 a Be-12 flew around a closed-circuit course carrying an 11,075lb (5,023kg) payload. Homing torpedoes, depth charges and sonobuoys are stored in the weapons bay, and air-to-surface missiles, unguided rockets and free-fall bombs are carried on the underwing pylons.

Below: Beriev Be-12, an ASW amphibian, is now being phased out.

Ilyushin Il-38 May

(CIS)

Type: LRMP aircraft (crew of 8-12).
Dimensions: Length 129.8ft (39.6m); span 122.7ft (37.4m); height 33.3ft (10.17m).
Weight: Empty 80,470lb (36,500kg); maximum 143,300lb (65,000kg).
Engines: 4 4,250ehp Ivchenko AI-20M single-shaft turboprops.
Performance: Maximum speed 380kt (704km/h) at altitude; patrol speed 174kt (322km/h); range 3,900nm (7,223km); patrol endurance 12hr.
Payload: Weapons bay for homing torpedoes, depth bombs, sonobuoys; maximum total load 15,432lb (7,000kg).

Like the US Navy's P-3 Orion which had its origins in the Lockheed Electra aircraft, the Ilyushin Il-38 May was developed from a turboprop passenger transport, in this case the Il-18 Coot. It is a new and purpose-built variant designed to incorporate the necessary sensors and weapons for ASW search and strike. Modifications to the basic Il-18 design include moving the wing forward to counter a shift in the centre of gravity caused by the weapons bay. A prominent search radar is fitted beneath the forward fuselage; the rear fuselage contains only sensors (including a MAD stinger in the tail) and sonobuoy launchers.

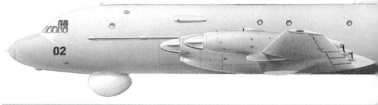

The fuselage has the same cross-section as that of the civil transport; the weapons bay, and consequently the payload, is thus small by Western standards, although there are four hardpoints under the wings for external stores. External inspection suggests an austere electronics fit, but CIS capabilities in this area should never be underestimated. There is a flight crew of four and a tactical crew of eight who are almost certainly assisted by an on-board computer. Offensive payload includes gravity bombs, depth charges, ASW torpedoes and nuclear depth bombs.

Some fifty-nine aircraft of this type are in service with the AV-MF, and five have been supplied to the Indian Navy, which took delivery in the late 1970s. Some Il-38s operated from Egyptian bases in the early 1970s in support of Soviet ASW operations in the eastern Mediterranean, and others deploy overseas from time to time. The most likely mission for the Il-38 in the event of war is in direct support of the CIS Navy's own ballistic missile submarine (SSBNs) in the Northern and Pacific fleet areas.

Below: An Ilyushin Il-38 long-range maritime patrol aircraft of the Indian Navy; five are currently in service.

Below: A CIS Navy Il-38 May out on patrol.

Tupolev Tu-142 (Bear-F)

(CIS)

Type: Very long-range ASW aircraft (crew of 7-12).
Dimensions: Length 162.40ft (49.5m); span 167.65ft (51.1m); height 39.76ft (12.12m).
Weight: Maximum 414,462lb (188,000kg).
Engines: 4 14,795ehp Kuznetsov NK-12MV turboprops.
Performance: Maximum speed 500kt (925km/h) at altitude; maximum unrefuelled combat radius 4,475nm (8,285km); service ceiling 44,300ft (13,500m); patrol endurance 28hr.
Payload: Depth bombs and torpedoes (estimated maximum weight 55,000lb (25,000kg)).

The Tupolev Tu-95 prototype flew in the summer of 1954 and was first seen by Western observers at the Tushino Air Display in July 1955; it was subsequently allocated the NATO reporting name of Bear. It has many claims to fame. It is the only swept-wing, propeller-driven aircraft ever to enter service; it is the largest *combat* aircraft in any air force; and it has been in continuous production for 35 years. It has excellent performance with a maximum speed of 500kt (925km/h) and a cruising speed of 384kt (711km/h); but it is its range which is truly exceptional with a combat *radius* of 4,475nm (8,285km), giving it an unrefuelled endurance of some 23 hours.

The Bear was designed to meet the Soviet requirement for a strategic bomber with sufficient range to reach targets in the USA. This first version — Bear-A — had a range of 8,000nm (14,800km) and carried a load of two nuclear bombs. The Bear-B was similar to Bear-A, but carried a Kangaroo air-to-surface missile, as did Bear-C. The primary role of Bear-D, first seen in 1967, is to provide targeting facilities for ship-launched anti-ship missiles, with a secondary role as a maritime reconnaissance platform. It carried no offensive armament and is fitted with numerous antennae and blisters for the additional electronic gear.

The next model was developed specifically for the Soviet Navy, for use in the long-range ASW role, and is believed to have entered service in 1970. The design is based on that of the Tu-95, but it is virtually a new aircraft and was

given the new designation Tu-142 by the Tupolev design bureau, although NATO merely gave it the next sub-type designation: Bear-F. The wing was completely redesigned to give twenty per cent greater lift, while the fuselage, although externally similar to that of the previous Tu-95, is longer and much "cleaner", with a lengthened pressure cabin inside. To cope with the increase in take-off weight, a new and stronger undercarriage was necessary and the housings for the main gear were enlarged to accommodate them.

The Bear-F has a large weapons bay which can accommodate depth bombs and torpedoes. Prior to 1992 there would have been nuclear warheads for both types of weapon, but following agreements with the USA these are no longer carried, conventional warheads only being employed. There are numerous sensors, including a very large search/surveillance radar beneath the fuselage, MAD housings on the end of the tailplane and sonobuoys in a large bay. One of the curious features of Soviet aircraft design has been the retention of gun turrets in many transport and bomber aircraft. The Bear-F is no exception to this, having a manned twin 20mm turret in the tail.

Fifteen of the original Bear-Fs were built, of which eight were later refurbished and sold to the Indian Navy. Production then switched to Bear-F Mod 1, which has revised electronics gear and reverts to the original, smaller undercarriage nacelles. The Bear-F Mod 2 (or Tupolev Tu-142M) has a completely redesigned cockpit which, combined with tilting the refuelling probe down by 4deg, gives the pilots a much better forward view. The fuselage is some 9in (22.9cm) longer and is much smoother than on previous versions.

In the Bear-F Mod 3 the streamlined pods on the tailplane have been replaced by a rearward-facing MAD fairing atop the fin, while the sonobuoy bay is narrower, but much longer. This version entered service in the early 1980s and appears to comprise both new production units and the modification of virtually all remaining aircraft of the previous Mod 1 and 2 types. The latest version, Mod 4, was first seen in 1986 and is essentially a Mod 3 with refinements and a new set of sensors in a faired cover under the nose. By 1992 some sixty-five Bear-Fs were in service, virtually all of which were either Mod 3 or Mod 4 standard.

Below: The Cold War may well be over, but CIS Navy aircraft such as this Tu-142 Bear-F Mod 3 ASW platform are still the subject of close scrutiny by Western powers' air defence fighters.

Dassault-Breguet Atlantique 2 (ATL2)

(International)

Type: Long-range maritime patrol aircraft (crew of 12).
Dimensions: Length 110.33ft (33.63m); span 122.77ft (37.42m); height 35.73ft (10.89m).
Weight: Empty 56,438lb (25,600kg); maximum 101,850lb (46,200kg).
Engines: 2 6,100ehp Rolls-Royce Tyne 21 two-shaft turboprops.
Performance: Maximum speed 355kt (658km/h) at altitude; patrol speed 170kt (315km/h); service ceiling 30,000ft (9,150m); patrol endurance 18hr; ferry range 4,400nm (8,150km).
Payload: Weapons bay for 8 homing torpedoes or 2 AM.39 air-to-surface missiles, depth charges and bombs; 4 underwing racks for up to 7,716lb (3,500kg) of stores including rockets, air-to-surface missiles or containers.

Most land-based ASW aircraft have been produced by converting existing designs, nowadays usually airliners. The Dassault-Breguet Atlantic was, however, specially designed for the ASW task, and a total of eighty-seven was produced for the naval air forces of France (forty), Germany (twenty), Italy (eighteen) and the Netherlands (nine) between 1964 and 1974. The type thus came very close to being the standard West European maritime patrol aircraft; indeed, it nearly succeeded in attracting an order from the Royal Air Force. The only export order — four machines for Pakistan — was met by selling three of the French Aéronavale machines and one sold back to the manufacturer by the Dutch.

By the mid-1970s a requirement for a follow-on design to replace both the Atlantic and the few remaining Lockheed P-2 Neptunes was identified, and it was decided that this could best be met by a new version of the Breguet aircraft. Design studies in 1977-78 led to the Atlantic Nouvelle Génération (NG) later known as the Atlantique 2 (ATL2). Changes to the airframe are limited to a number of improvements in sealing, bonding and anti-corrosion, particularly

to the elevator control system, failure of which was alleged to have caused several of the original aircraft to crash during maritime patrol operations.

The major changes are in the avionics and the chin turret of the SAT/TRT FLIR (forward-looking infra-red) sensor makes the new aircraft instantly recognisable. Atlantique 2 carries a Thompson-CSF Iguane I-band radar with a retractable ventral radome containing an integrated radar/IFF antenna and offering track-while-scan performance on up to 100 targets simultaneously. Antennae in the wing tips and in a fin-mounted pod feed the ARAR-13 ESM equipment, a passive receiver believed to cover the radar spectrum from 2.5 to 18.0GHz.

The prominent tail 'sting' houses a Crouzet MAD sensor which incorporates two detector elements whose ouputs are compared in order to measure the residual magnetic field of the aircraft, providing automatic compensation for changes due to different stores loads. All systems in the avionics installations are linked to a digital data bus, whilst a Thomson-CSF Cimesa digital computer processes and collates the tactical data from the sensors.

Armament carried in the weapons bay includes homing torpedoes, depth charges or AM.39 Exocet ASMs. A smaller bay further aft carries up to seventy-eight sonobuoys, usually a mixture of TSM 8010 and the newer, lighter and more capable TSM 8020.

Dassault-Breguet converted two existing Atlantic airframes as prototype Atlantique 2s, the first flying on 8 May 1981. The Aéronavale requires forty-two aircraft, delivery taking place between 1989 and 2001. Construction is being carried out by the same international consortium that built the original aircraft, i.e. Aérospatiale and Dassault-Breguet (France), Dornier and MBB (West Germany), Aeritalia (Italy) and Fokker, SABCA and Sonaca (Netherlands). No further orders for Atlantique 2 have been placed, and Germany and Italy are both upgrading their existing Atlantique 1 fleets. The Dutch transferred their five remaining Atlantics to the French Aéronavale in 1988 and now fly Lockheed P-3C Orions.

Below: The Atlantique 2 destined to lead the French Navy's fixed-wing ASW force well into the 21st Century.

BAe Nimrod MR.2P

(UK)

Type: Long-range maritime patrol aircraft (crew of 12).
Dimensions: Length 126.75ft (38.63m); span 114.8ft (35m); height 29.7ft (9.1m).
Weight: Empty 92,000lb (41,730kg); maximum 192,000lb (87,090kg).
Engines: 4 12,140lb (5,507kg) thrust Rolls-Royce Spey 250 2-shaft turbofans.
Performance: Maximum speed 500kt (926km/h); patrol speed 425kt /787km/h); service ceiling 42,000ft (12,800m); range 5,000nm (9,260km); patrol endurance 12hr.
Payload: Internal weapons bay for up to 6 Mk 46/Stingray homing torpedoes, depth bombs, sonobuoys; 2 wing pylons for Martel or AS.12 ASMs (some MR.2s fitted for AIM-9 Sidewinder AAMs).

Like many other long-range maritime patrol aircraft, the Nimrod is adapted from a civil airliner but, quite unlike any other in this role, it is powered by gas turbines instead of turboprops.

The Nimrod aircraft was derived from the de Havilland Comet 4, the direct descendant of the world's first jet airliner. A major advantage of jet propulsion is that the Nimrod has a high transit speed, and can thus react quickly to a submarine datum established by a broad-area detection system such as SOSUS, or by passive arrays towed by ships.

Forty-nine aircraft were built; of these, forty-three were to the MR.1 (ASW) standard, three were completed as R.1 Elint aircraft, and three were diverted from MR.1 to become trials aircraft for the AEW.3 programme. The original MR.1 was reliable, but its effectiveness in the ASW role was inhibited by its relatively austere avionics fit. This has been overcome by a major modernisation programme involving the installation of the EMI Searchwater radar, a Marconi AQS-901 acoustic processing and display system matched to the Barra sonobuoy, and a new Central Tactical Data system based on a Marconi 920 ATC digital computer. Thirty-four MR.1s were converted to this MR.2 standard. The ASW Nimrods serve with four RAF squadrons: No 42 at St Mawgan in south-west England, and Nos 120, 201 and 206 at RAF Kinloss in north-east Scotland. Further updating of the ASW Nimrods has been ruled out for technical reasons, because of the age of the airframes, although they will remain in active service until at least the year 2000.

Above: An excellent view of the Nimrod's internal weapons bay. Capable of delivering a hefty punch, the Nimrod can carry up to six homing torpedoes, as well as depth bombs. Another offensive capability includes anti-ship missiles carried on the wing pylons.

Below: The Nimrod MR.2, notice the air-to-air refuelling probe not carried on the earlier versions of the aircraft. The need for this capability was learned the hard way by the British during the Falklands War of 1982.

Lockheed P-3 Orion

(USA)

Type: Long-range maritime patrol aircraft (crew of 10).
Dimensions: Length 116.8ft (35.61m); span 99.7ft (30.37m); height 33.7ft (10.29m).
Weight: Empty 61,491lb (27,890kg); maximum 142,000lb (64,410kg).
Engines: 4 4,910shp Allison T56-14 single-shaft turboprops.
Performance: Maximum speed 410kt (761km/h); service ceiling 28,300ft (8,625m); range 4,500nm (8,334km); patrol endurance 16hr.
Payload: Weapons bay for Mk 46 torpedoes, depth bombs; 10 wing pylons for torpedoes, Harpoon ASMs, depth bombs, rocket pods, flares, mines, etc. Sonobuoys are carried internally and two Sidewinder AAMs are mounted on special pylons.

A 1957 US Navy requirement for an 'off the shelf' long-range maritime patrol aircraft based on an existing airframe to replace the ageing P-2 Neptune was met by Lockheed's proposed conversion of the Electra airliner, the P-3A Orion. The airframe was shortened by 12ft (3.65m), strengthened, equipped for weapons delivery and given increased fuel capacity. The avionics were initially those of the P-2, but improvements were made during the P-3A production run, with yet more in the P-3B (which also had more powerful engines).

The P-3C entered service in 1969, displaying few differences externally but with significant advances in ASW capability. Acoustic operators in earlier aircraft

tended to be overwhelmed by the quantity of sensor data, much of which was unusable, and to be handicapped by inadequate time in which to make decisions. This was resolved by introducing digital computers to record and analyse sensor data. As a result, acoustic operators in the P-3C monitor sixteen sonobuoys compared to eight in the P-3B and only four in the P-3A. The nine-sonobuoy launch chutes of the P-3A/B were increased to forty-eight externally-loaded chutes, plus one reloadable internal tube; low-light television (LLTV) replaced the searchlights; a FLIR dome replaced the chin gondola for cameras; improvements were made in passive electronic counter-measures (ECM), and installation of the AQS-81 MAD (from the forty-third P-3C) instantly doubled detection range.

The formidable capabilities of the P-3C are being further enhanced by a series of 'update' programmes. Update I (in service 1974) included the Omega navigation system, a new tactical display and a six-fold increase in computer memory. Update II (1978) included an improved acoustic recording system, provision for firing the Harpoon ASM, FLIR in place of LLTV, and a sonobuoy reference system similar to that of the S-3 Viking. The P-3C Update III was the last to enter service, the major change being the installation of the IBM UYS-1 acoustic signal processor, which has taken some time to get right as it affects virtually every other element of the aircraft's systems. About 80 P-3C Update II aircraft are being modified

Below: A fine study of one of thirteen P-3C Orions operated by the Royal Netherlands Navy, as it passes the ASW frigate _Kortenaer_ on patrol in the Atlantic Ocean. The Orions (all Upgrade II standard) were obtained as replacements for Dassault-Breguet Atlantics.

to Upgrade IV standard, with new equipment to enable them to detect and attack even quieter submarines.

The Electra was something of a failure as an airliner: only 170 were built, well short of the break-even figure. The Orion, however, has been an outstanding success, and deliveries now total 642 from the Lockheed lines alone, with Kawasaki in Japan producing a further 100. The US Navy operates twenty-six active squadrons of nine P-3Cs each, plus thirteen Naval Reserve squadrons with P-3A/Bs. P-3Bs are operated by New Zealand (five) and Norway (four); P-3Cs are operated by Australia (twenty), and the Netherlands (thirteen). Iran received six P-3Fs in the Shah's time, but only one or two are now serviceable. Japan is building ninety-seven P-3Cs under licence in addition to three delivered direct from Lockheed, whilst Canada has eighteen CP-140 Auroras, a variant of the P-3C built to Canadian specifications and incorporating the complete sensor and processing systems of the S-3A Viking.

Right: Loading a sonobuoy into one of the P-3 Orion's dispensing chutes located in the underfuselage. Up to 87 such sensors can be carried aboard a P-3C.

Below: A fine study of a US Navy P-3 Orion, with a particularly good view of the tail 'stinger' housing the extremely sensitive AN/ASQ-81 Magnetic Anomaly Detector.

Lockheed   S-3/ES-3   Viking
(USA)

Type: Carrier-based ASW aircraft (crew of 4).
Dimensions: Length 53.3ft (16.26m); span 68.7ft (20.93m); height 22.75ft (6.93m).
Weight: Empty 26,783lb (12,149kg); maximum 52,539lb (23,832kg).
Engines: 2 9,275lb (4,207kg) thrust General Electric TF34-400 turbofans.
Performance: Maximum speed 440kt (814km/h) at sea level; service ceiling 35,000ft (10,670m); ferry range 3,000nm (5,556km); mission range 2,000nm (3,705km); mission endurance 9hr.
Payload: 2/4 Mk 46 homing torpedoes; 2/4 depth bombs in internal weapons bays; 2 wing pylons for Harpoon missiles, bombs, rockets or fuel tanks.

Designed to replace the Grumman S-2 Tracker in the carrier-borne fixed-wing role for the US Navy, the Lockheed S-3 Viking is a very sophisticated aircraft equipped with the most advanced detection and data processing capabilities. Sensors include a high resolution radar (APS-116) for maritime reconnaissance, MAD (ASQ-81 (V)), FLIR, and sixty sonobuoys for submarine detection. Behind the pilot and co-pilot sit the Tactical Coordinator (TACCO) and the Sensor Operator (SENSO). The primary data display is the ASA-82 system, which serves as a

real-time link between the four-man crew and the various surface and underwater sensors. Information is stored, updated, refreshed and selectively displayed by the AYK-30 on-board digital computer.

The initial production order of 187 aircraft was completed by FY77. From the mid-1970s, fixed-wing squadrons, each of ten S-3A Vikings, were added to the air groups of all the US Navy's multi-purpose aircraft carriers, except for the two older ships of the Midway class. There was some initial criticism of the additional maintenance load imposed by the S-3A, but its ability to react quickly and effectively to a distant underwater contact has proved invaluable.

160 aircraft are being upgraded to S-3B standard, which involves an increase in acoustic and radar processing capabilities, expanded electronic support measures (ESM), a new sonobuoy receiver system (ARR-78(V)) and the Harpoon anti-ship missile. This last will, of course, add considerably to the carriers' already strong attack potential. There is also an ES-3A version, which is fitted with special electronic equipment to enable it to monitor potentially hostile fleets from beyond the horizon. This carries no less than sixty external antennae, indicating a very complex and sophisticated electronic fit.

Below: A pair of S-3A Vikings, the only fixed-wing, jet-powered, carrier-based ASW platform in service today. Torpedoes, missiles, bombs, depth charges, mines and rocket pods can all be carried.

ASW Helicopters

Almost from the machine's inception, the possibility of using the helicopter at sea was in the minds of designers and naval staffs alike. The US Navy was using Sikorsky R-4s at sea in 1943, but for the next ten years or so their role was limited to reconnaissance and liaison. Gradually, however, the potential of the helicopter as an ASW platform began to be realised. The US Navy went off at a tangent for some years with DASH, a radio-controlled drone helicopter carrying a torpedo, but it was the Royal Canadian Navy which pioneered the use of manned helicopters from a flight deck on the sterns of destroyers and frigates — a practice which is now almost universal. Initially, these simply carried torpedoes to the area dictated by the parent ship's sensors, but as sensors and processors have become smaller and lighter, ASW heliccopters have become increasingly autonomous. Today's larger ASW helicopters, such as the SH-3 Sea King, are highly capable ASW systems in their own right. Indeed, so capable are these types that a new type of ship has been created — the helicopter carrier — whose sole reason for existence is to act as a platform for such very effective sub-hunters. The Sea King first entered service with the US Navy in the early 1960s and has been a dominant force ever since. It is active with every nation equipped with carriers bar France and the Commonwealth of Independent States. Today's Sea Kings are now giving way to a range of other helicopters such as the American SH-60F Seahawk and the European EH. 101.

Helicopters hunt submarines using either dunking sonar or sonobuoys. Dunking sonar is an effective short-range system, although the active systems are limited in performance by the size of the helicopter carrying them. The major shortcoming is that the helicopter must hover close to the surface while 'dunking', which consumes much fuel and prevents the aircraft from being used for other roles at the same time. Sonobuoys are more effective and release the helicopter from the hovering problem, but because they are expendable they become very expensive — the last admitted US annual expenditure on sonobuoys was $74 million, a price well beyond the reach of most navies. Helicopters also employ magnetic anomaly detectors (MAD), a useful passive system for confirming a target's presence. They usually deploy the magnetometer in a 'bird' towed behind the aircraft on a cable, although a Canadian company is now offering a built-in design for helicopters.

The primary ASW weapon for helicopters is the torpedo, which can be dropped very close to the target. Depth charges can also be carried. Nuclear depth bombs have been carried by certain nations' ASW helicopters in the past, but this practise has now ceased.

Below: The helicopter's ASW role was slow to be realised, but with the advent of smaller, lighter avionics, it soon became apparent that a ship-borne helicopter could become a powerful and independent ASW system. These two SH-3 Sea Kings — one of the first types to be used in the ASW role — are seen in markings of the Royal Australian Navy.

Kamov Ka-25 Hormone

(CIS)

Type: Shipborne ASW helicopter (crew of 4-5).
Dimensions: Fuselage length 32ft (9.75m); main rotor diameter 51.7ft (15.75m); height 17.6ft (5.37m).
Weight: Empty 10,500lb (4,765kg); maximum 16,534lb (7,506kg).
Engines: T20 990hp Glushenkov GTD-3BM free-turbine turboshafts.
Performance: Maximum speed 113kt (209km/h); service ceiling 11,000ft (3,350m); range 350nm (650km); mission endurance 1½-2hr.
Payload: 1-2 15.75 in (400mm) homing torpedoes, depth bombs in internal weapons bay; maximum total load 2,200lb (1,000kg).

Below: The romantic setting almost disguises the lethal role of this Ka-25 Hormone ASW helicopter out on a sunset patrol.

Left: Ka-25 Hormone-A ASW helicopter. Note prominent chin surface search radar and the nose-mounted 'Homeguide' Yagi antennas. The inverted flower-pot housing on the tail boom is assumed to be an electro-optical sensor, precise role unclear.

The untidy and inelegant appearance of the Kamov Ka-25 Hormone tends to disguise the fact that the ingenious Kamov design bureau has produced a highly effective shipborne helicopter. The twin turbines provides a lot of power and in combination with the coaxial rotors give high lift; furthermore, the rotor configuration does away with the long tail boom and dangerous tail-rotor found in most rotary-wing designs. The overall result is a competent and versatile machine. The Ka-25 is the current standard CIS shipboard helicopter. It first flew in 1960, and some 460 have been built in a production run which listed from 1966 to 1975. About 100 remain in service: India (five), Syria (five) Yugoslavia (eight) and the remainder with the CIS Navy.

Three versions have been identified. Hormone-A is the basic ASW version equipped with a chin-mounted search radar, a towed MAD sensor and a dunking sonar. Most examples are of this version. Additional sensors have been added during the last decade, but the type still lacks night-vision equipment and the ability to operate its sonar in all weathers. Some aircraft have a small fairing mounted immediately below the centre tail fin, but unlike that on the Mi-14 Haze (qv) this cannot be assumed to be a float. A small cylindrical housing (resembling an inverted flower pot) is mounted above the tail boom of many aircraft. This has a transparent upper section and is presumably some sort of electro-optical sensor. Hormone-A carries a crew comprising a pilot, a co-pilot and two or three systems operators.

A small weapons bay in the cabin floor carries a payload which can consist of combinations of sonobuoys, ASW torpedoes, depth charges, nuclear depth-bombs or other stores. Some of the more recent aircraft also have a rectangular underfuselage weapons container, and most have stores racks on the starboard side of the fuselage. In addition, there is evidence of an upgrading programme to fit small 'fire-and-forget' missiles. Most aircraft have their four undercarriage wheels enclosed in inflatable pontoons, which in turn are surmounted by the inflation bottles.

Hormone-B is an anti-ship missile aircraft, recognisable by its larger, more curved chin radome and an additional retractable ventral radome. This aircraft is used to acquire targets for the SS-N-12 long-range ASM. The final version, Hormone-C, is a utility and search-and-rescue (SAR) aircraft.

Right: A busy flight-deck scene aboard a Moskva class carrier. The two aircraft on the deck are Hormone-As, but the radome of the aircraft behind suggests that it is probably a Hormone-B, which is the electronic warfare version.

Above: Kamov Ka-25 Hormone ASW helicopter on the flight-deck of a Kanin class destroyer. The sailors appear to be doing maintenance on the nose radar, with the radome lying on the deck. This aircraft also has the inflatable pontoons on all wheels to give flotation in the event of an emergency landing. Note the complex rotor-head.

Left. This profile shows a standard Kamov Ka-25 Hormone-A but without the inflatable pontoons on the wheels. An interesting feature of this design is that the wheels can be raised vertically in flight to prevent radar echoes, which would degrade equipment performance.

Kamov Ka-27 Helix

(CIS)

Type: Shipborne ASW helicopter (crew of 3-4).
Dimensions: Fuselage length 37ft (11.3m); main rotor diameter 52.2ft (15.9m); height 17.7ft (5.44m).
Weight: Maximum 24,250lb (11,000kg).
Engines: 2 2,225shp Isotov TV-3-117V turboshafts.
Performance: Maximum speed 135kt (250km/h); service ceiling 19,685ft (6,000m); range 432nm (800km); mission endurance 4.5 hours.
Payload: 7,716lb (3,500kg) maximum; depth bombs and/or 2 torpedoes.

The Kamov Ka-27 Helix continues the Kamov design bureau's successful formula for a shipborne ASW helicopter, with twin co-axial rotors which remove the need for a tail rotor mounted on a lengthy tail boom. The Ka-27 was first seen during Exercise ZAPAD-81 (West-81) in the Baltic, when two helicopters of the type (one in civilian colours) operated from the new Soviet destroyer *Udaloy*. Although its cabin is slightly larger than that of the Hormone, the Helix is clearly intended to be compatible with ships capable of operating the former. Some components seem identical to the older type, but more powerful engines are

fitted, whilst the rotor blades fold in the same way but are of a slightly different form. There is a box under the tail boom for the MAD 'bird' and there are boxes either side of the cabin which are assumed to be for sonobuoys. There are two known ASW versions of this helicopter, the Ka-27 (as described above) and the externally identical Ka-28, which is specifically for export; both are given the NATO designation Helix-A. The Ka-27 is replacing the Hormone in the CIS Navy, with some ninety now in service.

It seems possible that the Helix may overcome one of the shortcomings of the Hormone and be capable of all-weather and night sonar dipping operations. It may also be able to carry two of the new 17.7in (450mm) electric-powered torpedoes. Other weapons include depth charges. Other naval versions are the Helix-B, which is used for commando transport and missile guidance, and the Helix-D, which has simpler equipment and is used for SAR and plane guard duties. The Kamov Ka-32 or Helix-C is a demilitarised version of the Ka-27 for civilian use, mainly as a flying-crane.

Below: The basic ASW version of the Ka-27 is Helix-A, in service since the early 1980s. Prominent beneath this version's nose is a 360deg search radar housing, used in conjunction with a dipping sonar housed in a compartment behind the clamshell doors at the rear of the fuselage pod. Over 100 Helix-As are in service.

Mil Mi-14 Haze

(CIS)

Type: Land-based ASW helicopter (crew of 4-5).
Dimensions: Fuselage length 60ft (18.3m); main rotor diameter 69.9ft (21.3m); height 22.75ft (6.93m).
Weight: Empty 17,650lb (8,000kg); maximum 30,865lb (14,000kg).
Engines: 2 1,950shp Isotov TV3-117A free-turbine turboshafts.
Performance: Maximum speed 124kt (230km/h); service ceiling 11,500ft (3,500m); maximum range 612nm (1,135km/h); maximum endurance 5hr 56min.
Payload: Homing torpedoes; depth bombs; possibly ASMs.

The prototype Mil Mi-14 Haze first flew in 1973. Clearly designed for ASW operations, it was at first thought in the West to be intended for the larger ASW ships, but in fact, it is only intended for operation from land bases. In creating this ASW helicopter for the ex-Soviet Navy the Mil bureau has adopted the well-proven configuration of the Mil Mi-8. The fuselage has been remodelled with a boat-hull bottom which, in conjunction with sponsons on either side of the fuselage, gives a degree of amphibious capability. There is, however, a large radome under the nose which could be damaged during a landing on water, which suggests that the amphibious capability may be for emergencies rather than for routine operations. The tricycle landing-gear is similar to that of the Mi-8 except that it is retractable.

The most conspicious of the sensors is a 360° search radar, its antenna in a chin-mounted radome. A towed MAD bird is fitted at the rear of the fuselage. The prominent box under the tail-boom houses the antenna for a Doppler radar, while the small, pod-like object under the tail-boom is a float to prevent the

Below: A CIS Navy Mi-14 Haze approaches a Kashin class destroyer.

Above: The box beneath the tail boom contains a Doppler radar.

blades of the tail rotor from striking the water. Weapons are carried in an internal bay in the bottom of the hull and sonobuoys are launched down two chutes at the rear of the hull.

There are three versions of this helicopter. The Mil Mi-14PL Haze-A is the basic ASW version, described above. The Mi-14BT Haze-B is a mine countermeasures (MCM) aircraft and the Mi-14PS Haze-C is for search-and-rescue duties. Some 240 Mi-14s have been built, of which the bulk serve with the CIS Navy. Others are in service with Bulgaria (ten), Cuba (five), Libya (twenty-five), Poland (eleven), Syria (twelve), Yugoslavia (ten). A number operated by the navy of the former German Democratic Republic were taken over by the Bundesmarine, but are not being operated and may be sold or scrapped.

Aérospatiale Super Frelon

France

Type: Shipborne/land-based ASW helicopter (crew of 5).
Dimensions: Fuselage length 63.6ft (19.4m); main rotor diameter 62ft (18.9m); height 21.9ft (6.66m).
Weight: Empty 15,130lb (6,863kg); maximum 28,660lb (13,000kg).
Engines: 3 1,570shp Turboméca Turmo $IIIC_6$ turboshafts.
Performance: Maximum speed 148kt (275km/h); service ceiling 10,325ft (3,150m); range 440nm (815km); mission endurance 4hr.
Payload: 4 Mk 44/46 homing torpedoes or 2 AM.39 ASMs.

Until the arrival of the EH.101 Merlin, the Aerospatiale SA.321G Super Frelon was the largest helicopter to have been built in Western Europe. Production in France for the French forces and for export has ended, but the type is still in production in China. It was derived from Aérospatiale's SA.3200 Frelon but incorporated technology 'brought in' from other companies: the main lift and tail rotors and their drive systems were designed with assistance from Sikorsky, who also helped with the boat-shaped hull; and Fiat assisted with the main gearbox and power transmission.

Twenty-four SA.321G Super Frelons were built for the Aéronavale, of which twelve still serve in the ASW role and four as transports. A number of the ASW version have operated from the carriers *Clémenceau* and *Foch* in recent years. The SA.321 is also responsible for ASW operations in support of French ballistic missile submarines (SNLE). These duties include 'de-lousing' the SNLEs as they leave port to start their patrols. The SA.321Gs generally operate in groups of up to four aircraft, with one employing its Sylphe panoramic dunking sonar for listening while the others make their attacks. Equipment includes a 360° search radar, doppler navigation radar, dunking sonar and up to four homing torpedoes. French Navy aircraft were updated in the 1980s, the Héraclès ORB radar being replaced by the more powerful Héraclès II version which doubles the range and is also compatible with the AM.39 Exocet anti-ship missile.

The Libyan Air Force operates twelve SA.321Ms in the ASW/SAR roles. Iraq operates some thirteen Super Frelons armed with Exocet in the ship attack role. The People's Republic of China purchased thirteen SA.321Gs from France for ASW use and has now set up its own production line at the Changhe Aircraft Factory in Jiangxi, under the designation Zhishengji-8 (Z-8). The programme was started as long ago as 1975 and progress has been very slow, but type approval was eventually given in 1989 and it now appears that the type is in full-scale production.

Above: A Super Frelon of the French Aéronavale with its dunking sonar deployed. These helicopters have had their onboard systems upgraded, but the fleet is showing its age and needs replacing.

Above: An SA.321G moments after lifting its Sylphe panoramic dunking sonar from the sea. Note also the large nose-mounted Héraclès II search radar radome.

EHI EH-101
(International)

Type: Shipborne/land-based ASW helicopter (crew of 4).

Dimensions: Fuselage length 56.75ft (17.3m); main rotor diameter 61ft (18.5m); height (rotors turning) 17.1ft (5.21m).

Weight: Empty 20,500lb (9,298kg); maximum loaded 28,660lb (13,000kg).

Engines: 3 1,437shp General Electric T700-GE-401A turboshafts.

Performance: Maximum speed (sea level) 167kt (309km/h); range (classified); endurance (classified).

Payload: 4 homing torpedoes, and/or anti-ship missiles and depth bombs.

A series of British MoD(N) feasibility studies under Naval Staff Requirement 6646 (NSR.6646) were carried out during 1974/77 to define how a Sea King replacement (SKR) would operate and what sensors and performance standards it would require against the fast, deep-diving Soviet submarines anticipated in the 1990s. These showed that the best results in such an ASW role would be obtained by a helicopter having a high all-round performance, particularly long range and good endurance, and operating in the autonomous mode. The best sensors for the Atlantic Ocean and North Sea were found to be dropped sonobuoys, backed up by radar, radar intercept equipment and MAD. As happens elsewhere, however, all these sensors would produce such a volume of data that an automated handling system would be needed. The aircraft designed

to answer these requirements was designated the Westland WG.34, a machine very slightly smaller, but much more powerful than the current Sea King; it was accepted in 1978. The Italian firm Agusta decided to participate in the project in 1980, and the combined firm of Elicotteri Helicopter Industries (EHI) was formed. Supply will be from single-source manufacturers, but there will be two assembly lines: one in Britain, the other in Italy.

In the ASW role the normal crew will be pilot (the naval version is designed for single-pilot operation), observer, acoustic systems operator and flight crewman. Equipment includes GEC Avionics AQS-903 acoustic processor system, Ferranti Blue Kestrel search radar (in the prominent chin-mounted radome) Racal ESM and Omega. Comprehensive secure communications and the JTIDS digital data link will be installed.

The version for the Royal Navy is designated the EH-101 Merlin and fifty have been ordered for operation from Invincible class carriers, Type 23 frigates and RFAs. The Italian Navy has ordered forty-two which will operate from the carrier *Giuseppe Garibaldi*, cruisers and the larger destroyers. Both navies will also operate the aircraft from shore bases. Canada has selected the EH 101 to replace its Sea Kings on board its destroyers and frigates and is expected to place a firm order for thirty-five in due course for delivery in the mid-to-late 1990s.

Below: Representing the future shape of the Royal Navy's heliborne ASW force is the EH-101 Merlin, fifty of which have been ordered to replace the Westland Sea Kings now in service. The Merlins will operate from Duke and Invincible class vessels, and land bases.

Agusta-Bell AB.212ASW

(Italy/USA)

Type: Shipborne ASW helicopter (crew of 3-4).
Dimensions: Fuselage length 45.9ft (14m); main rotor diameter 48ft (14.6m); height 12.8ft (3.9m).
Weight: Empty 7,540lb (3,420kg); maximum 11,200lb (5,080kg).
Engines: 1 1,875shp United Aircraft of Canada PT6T-3 Turbo Twin Pac.
Performance: Maximum speed 106kt (196km/h); service ceiling 14,200ft (4,330m); range 315nm (584km); mission endurance 3hr.
Payload: 2 torpedoes or 2 anti-ship missiles.

Agusta-Bell developed the AB.204 from the basic Bell UH-1 utility helicopter for use by the Regia Aeronautica. An ASW variant — AB.204AS — was also developed, for use from a series of anti-submarine cruisers and frigates built for the Italian Navy during the 1960s. These aircraft worked in pairs, one being fitted with an AQS-13B dunking sonar and the other with a pair of Mk 44/46 homing torpedoes.

The AB.212 is similar in overall dimensions to its predecessor but represents a great increase in capability, not the least being that it can operate in the ASW role autonomously, whereas the earlier type could only operate as part of a team of two. A more powerful search radar is fitted in a prominent radome on the cabin roof, and sonobuoys are carried in addition to the AQS-13B dunking sonar. Two anti-ship missiles (ASMs) can be carried for the surface attack role, and the TG-2 system enables the AB.212AS to provide mid-course guidance for ship-launched Otomat SSMs. The AB.212 is unique among ship-borne

Right: The radome for the AB.212ASW's Ferranti Seaspray long-range search radar is clearly visible atop the helicopter's cockpit roof.

Below: Retention of landing skids on an ASW helicopter is unique to the AB.212ASW. Note the inflatable pontoons for on-water landings.

helicopters in that it has a large-diameter twin-bladed rotor, all others having smaller diameter, faster rotating three-, four- or five-bladed rotors. Also, the AB.212 has a skid undercarriage, whereas all others have wheels, which are not only easier to move around on the deck but also incorporate more effective shock-absorbing systems to cope with the loads when landing on a heaving deck. Nevertheless, the AB.212 is based on the well-proven and very reliable Bell UH-1 series of helicopters and has won a good number of export orders.

This design is unique to Agusta-Bell, and there is no equivalent in the range offered by the parent company in the USA. Sixty have been built for the Italian Navy, with further machines ordered by Greece (twelve), Iraq (five), Peru (six), Turkey (twelve) and Venezuela (six).

Westland/Aérospatiale Lynx

(International)

Type: Shipborne ASW/strike helicopter (crew of 2).
Dimensions: Fuselage length 39.6ft (12.1m); main rotor diameter 42ft (12.8m); height 11.5ft (3.5m).
Weight: Empty 7,370lb (3,343kg); maximum 10,500lb (4,763kg).
Engines: 2 1,120shp Rolls-Royce Gem 41-1 triple-shaft turbines.
Performance: Maximum speed 145kt (269km/h); service ceiling 12,000ft (3,658m); range 320nm (593km); mission endurance (max) 2hr 29min.
Payload: (ASW) 2 Mk 46 or Stingray homing torpedoes, or 2 Mk 11 depth bombs; (surface strike) 4 AS.12 or Sea Skua ASMs.

Many modern ASW helicopters have carried out search operations against unknown, and at least sometimes potentially hostile, targets, but the Lynx is one of the very few to have actually attacked a submarine in anger. In the 1982 South Atlantic War, during the reoccupation of South Georgia, Royal Navy Lynxes caught the Argentine submarine *Sante Fé* on the surface and attacked her with wire-guided missiles and free-flight rockets, forcing her to beach and surrender.

Developed by Westland as part of the Anglo-French helicopter deal, the Lynx is built in 70/30 partnership with Aérospatiale of France. The standard version serving with the Royal Navy is the HAS.3, which is fitted with Ferranti Sea Spray search radar and a passive sonobuoy processor. Unlike the US Navy's LAMPS,

the Lynx is intended to operate autonomously in the ASW role. It thus carries not only all the necessary on-board sensors (Bendix AQS-18 or Alcatel DUAV-4 'dunking sonar', ASQ-18 MAD 'bird') but also weaponry such as Mk 44 or 46 lightweight homing torpedoes or Sea Skua missiles. During the South Atlantic operations the Sea Skua missiles were launched in near-blizzard conditions, scoring five hits out of five.

The Royal Navy received sixty of the original ASW version (HAS.2). Next came the HAS.3 with more powerful engines, of which thirty were new-builds and fifty-three upgraded from Mk.2s. Current plans are to upgrade the entire fleet of HAS.3s to HAS.8 standard, with even more powerful engines and improved on-board avionics.

The French Navy procured twenty-six HAS.2 (FN), followed by 14 Mk.4s, which were equivalent to the Royal Navy's Mk.2 and Mk.3, respectively. Other navies to have taken delivery of ASW Lynxes are: Argentina (two Mk.23); Brazil (nine Mk.21); Denmark (eight Mk.80, two Mk.90); Germany (nineteen Mk.88); Netherlands (six Mk.25); Nigeria (three Mk.89); Portugal (five Super Lynx); and South Korea (twelve Super Lynx).

Current development effort is centred on the Super Lynx, which was initially developed for export; the equivalent for the Royal Navy being the Mk.8.

Below: Caught moments after lift-off from HMS *Alacrity*'s helipad, this Royal Navy Lynx HAS.3 totes a pair of Sea Skua semi-active homing torpedoes on its port-side pylons. The protruberance atop the nose houses MIR-2 Orange Crop ESM passive receivers.

Kaman SH-2 Seasprite

(USA)

Type: Shipborne ASW helicopter (crew of 3).
Dimensions: Fuselage length 40.5ft (12.3m); main rotor diameter 44.25ft (13.5m); height (rotors turning) 15.0ft (4.58m).
Weight: Empty 7,600lb (3,447kg); maximum loaded 13,500lb (6,124kg).
Engines: 3 1,723shp General Electric T700-GE-401A turboshafts.
Performance: Maximum speed (sea level) 138kt (256km/h); range 478nm (885km); endurance 5hr.
Payload: 2 homing torpedoes.
Data are for SH-2G; earlier versions differ slightly

This exceptionally neat helicopter was initially powered by a single turbine engine mounted close under the rotor hub, and was able to carry a wide range of loads, including nine passengers and two crew. The main units of the tailwheel undercarriage retracted fully. Some 190 machines were delivered, and all were later converted to have two T58 engines in nacelles on each side of the main rotor housing. All SH-2s were drastically converted in the 1970s to serve in the Light Airborne Multi-Purpose System (LAMPS) programme for anti-submarine and anti-missile defence.

The SH-2F (LAMPS Mk 1) has more than two tons of special equipment, including a powerful chin-mounted radar, sonobuoys, MAD gear, ECM, new navigation and communications systems and Mk 44 or 46 torpedoes. Though

only the 'interim LAMPS' platform, the SH-2F was a substantial programme. The first of eighty-eight new SH-2Fs became operational in mid-1973 and all had been delivered by the end of the decade. Kaman then rebuilt the earlier models still in service to the new standard, and this work was completed in March 1982. Meanwhile, to meet pressing requirements, the production line was reopened in 1981 for a further run of eighteen aircraft.

Sensors fitted to the SH-2F include a Canadian Marconi LN-66HP surveillance radar with its antenna mounted in a prominent radome immediately under the nose. Other sensors are the Texas Instruments AQS-81 towed MAD and ALR-66 ESM receiver. The aircraft entered service using the SSQ-41 (passive) and SSQ-47 (active) sonobuoys, but these were replaced by the newer Difar and Dicass models. Normal armament is a pair of homing torpedoes.

Latest model is the SH-2G, which features many improvements including the replacement of the old General Electric T-58 turbofan by the newer and much more efficient T-700. The US Navy is acquiring 103 of this model, many by conversion of earlier aircraft, but some by new construction. This remarkable helicopter first flew in July 1959 and thirty years later still has plenty of life left. Several countries have expressed an interest in buying export versions, but so far Pakistan is the only country to have placed a firm order. Six were ordered in 1989 (with an option on three more), of which three had been delivered by the end of 1991.

Below: A pair of recently-fired sonobuoys fall away from an SH-2F Seasprite armed with a Mk 46 torpedo. Returns from the sonobuoys will be monitored by the sensor operator in the Seasprite's cabin.

Sikorsky SH-3 Sea King

(International)

Type: Shipborne/land-based ASW helicopter (crew of 4).

Dimensions: Fuselage length 54.75ft (16.7m); main rotor diameter 62ft (18.9m); height 16.8ft (5.1m).

Weight: Empty 11,865lb (5,382kg); maximum 21,000lb (9,525kg).

Engines: 2 1,500shp General Electric T58-GE-100 turboshafts.

Performance: Maximum speed 144kt (267km/h); service ceiling 12,200ft (3,720m); range 630nm (1,166km); mission endurance 4½hr.

Payload: Up to 4 Mk 44, Mk 46, Whithead A 224 AS Stingray homing torpedoes, or 4 depth bombs/charges.

More than three decades after its first flight, the Sea King is still in production, more than 770 having been built by Sikorsky and a further 500-plus built under licence by Agusta (Italy), Mitsubishi (Japan), and Westland (UK). These latter are much modified from the original and are described separately below.

The Sea King started life as the HSS-2 ASW helicopter and entered service with the US Navy in the early 1960s as the SH-3A; 255 were built for the USN, with a further forty-one built in Canada (as the CH-124) and seventy-three in Japan (as the S-61B). The next version for the US Navy was the SH-3D, powered by the T58-GE-10. This was fitted with a Bendix AQS-13 dunking sonar and could carry sonobuoys and weapons such as homing torpedoes, depth charges and depth bombs; seventy-two were built for the US Navy, twenty-two for Spain.

The current SH-3H has new ASW equipment and all remaining USN SH-3As, SH-3Ds and SH-3Gs are being brought up to this standard. The US Navy currently operates fifteen squadrons in the carrier-based ASW role, each with six SH-3D/Hs

One of a long line of Sikorsky aircraft to be built under licence by Westland, the British version is based on the US Navy's SH-3 airframe but 'under the skin' is a very different machine, intended to operate independently of surface ships when hunting and attacking submarines. This requirement led Westland to install a complete tactical centre and a full range of sensors. All Westland Sea Kings are fitted with two Rolls-Royce Gnome turboshafts, based on the General Electric T58 used in the SH-3.

The original Sea King HAS.1 ordered for the Royal Navy flew in 1969, and fifty-six were delivered by mid-1972. Twenty-one HAS.2s were then built, and all HAS.1s modified to the new standard; all these were later brought up to HAS.5

standard. A search radar is fitted, the antenna being housed under a prominent 'hump' on the cabin roof behind the engine-housing; latest versions are fitted with the MEL Supersearcher. The total orders for all versions of the Westland Sea King/Commando stood at 324 in 1991, which, apart from the Royal Navy, have also been supplied to Australia, Egypt, Germany, India and Pakistan.

The Sea King has been produced in Italy by Agusta since 1967, under the designation ASH-3. This is virtually identical to the US Navy version, apart from minor modifications, such as increased strengthening of some parts and uprated engines. Some twenty-five ASH-3D/Hs are in service with the Italian Navy; most of these serve aboard the ASW carrier *Giuseppe Garibaldi*, while the others are shore-based. Agusta has also exported a number, including four to Argentina, and seven each to Brazil and Iran. Agusta has also received an order from the US Navy to produce modification kits to bring its Sea Kings up to SH-3H standard, since Sikorsky production has long since ended.

In Japan, production has been undertaken by Mitsubishi. The total order for the Japanese defence forces was 185, of which some 105 were ASW versions. Production has now switched to the Mitsubishi SH-60J Seahawk.

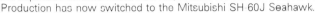

Above: An Italian Navy ASH-3H Sea King dropping a homing torpedo. Note the chin radome for the SMA/APS-707 radar, which has been specially designed to feed target data to the long-range anti-ship missiles which can also be carried by this versatile helicopter.

Left: A Royal Navy Sea King Mk 5 carrying homing torpedos. Built under licence by Westland, the Sea King has been operated by the Royal Navy since 1969. Its role is now being taken by the introduction of the EH-101 Merlin, a helicopter which will also serve with the Italian and Canadian navies.

Sikorsky SH-60B/J Seahawk & SH-60F Oceanhawk

(USA)

Type: Shipborne ASW helicopter (crew of 3).
Dimensions: Fuselage length 50ft (15.2m); main rotor diameter 53.7ft (16.4m); height 17.2ft (5.2m).
Weight: Empty 13,648lb (6,191kg); maximum 21,884lb (9,926kg).
Engines: 2 1,900shp General Electric T700-GE-401C turboshafts.
Performance: Maximum speed 126kt (234km/h); service ceiling 18,500ft (5,639m); mission endurance 3½hr.
Payload: 2 Mk 46 homing torpedoes and 2 AGM-119B Penguin Mk 2 Mod 7 ASMs.

The Sikorsky SH-60B Seahawk is the basis of the US Navy's LAMPS III ASW system for operation from cruisers, destroyers and frigates. The aircraft is a variant of the US Army's UH-60A, developed under the Utility Tactical Transport Aircraft System (UTTAS) project. The Navy aircraft has different landing gear from the Army model and folding systems for the main rotor and tail, both of which are required for operations from small ships at sea. The aircraft features an advanced rotor design and an engine built from individual modules.

The primary LAMPS mission is ASW, and the aircraft carries an extensive avionics suite developed by an industrial team headed by IBM. The main sensors are a Texas Instruments APS-124 search radar in the forward section of the fuselage, an ASQ-81 towed MAD system, a UYS-1 acoustic processor and an ALQ-142 ESM system. Two Mk 46 lightweight torpedoes can be carried on pylons, and a 25-tube sonobuoy launcher is fitted on the port side of the fuselage.

The LAMPS III system is ship-based: overall control remains with the parent ship, which also processes data from the helicopter's own sensors. SH-60B operations are monitored by an acoustic sensor operator (ASO) in the ship's sonar room, and a remote radar operator (REMRO) and an electronic warfare operator (EWO) in the ship's Combat Information Centre (CIC). There is also an air tactical control officer (ATACO) who co-ordinates the activities of the three operators and who is, in effect, the tactical mission commander. The SH-60B has a crew of three: pilot, airborne tactical officer (ATO) — who monitors the ship's tactical direction of the mission — and sensor operator.

A new ASW version, the SH-60F Oceanhawk, provides close-in ASW protection for US Navy carrier groups. In this version all the LAMPS gear has been removed, as has the equipment related to frigate operations.

Australia has ordered sixteen SH-60Bs. The type is also being produced by Mitsubishi in Japan as the SH-60J, against an order for some 100 from the Japanese Maritime Self-Defence Force

Below: An SH-60B Seahawk Lamps III helicopter on patrol close to her parent ship, USS *Crommelin*. The red-and-yellow unit carried on the mid-fuselage is an ASQ-81 Magnetic Anomaly Detection "bird", which is streamed aft of the helicopter when in use.

ASW Weapons Systems

Spearfish (UK)

The Royal Navy introduced the Tigerfish torpedo in 1980 after a long and troubled development programme, but it has not proved too successful in service and is, in any case, too slow for modern underwater targets. It will be replaced by Spearfish. This new torpedo is a 4,077lb (1,850kg), dual-purpose missile and is reputed to have a speed of some 70kt near the surface, although this reduces with depth, and a range of some 13.1 miles (21km). It uses a pump-jet propulsor, powered by a Sundstrand turbine engine, which uses mixed hydrogen-amonium perchlorate/OTTO fuel to give the high power output necessary for such a high speed. In action, Spearfish is launched at a depth of some 656ft (200m) and then ascends to about 164ft (50m), where it runs at about 28kt in the general direction of the target under control from the submarine using wire-guidance. It then starts a passive search until it finds a target, when it switches to the active mode for a high-speed attack. It incorporates a special sonar-imaging device to avoid being misled by decoys launched from the target submarine. The shaped-charge warhead includes some 660lb (300kg) of Torpex and is intended to defeat the very fast, deep-diving and inherently strong CIS Navy submarines, such as the Alfa, Sierra and Akula classes. Spearfish, which is also known as Naval Staff Requirement 7525 (NSR 525), is due to enter service in the mid-1990s.

L5 Multipurpose Torpedo (France)

This torpedo is in service with the French and Belgian Navies. It is powered by silver-zinc batteries and has a speed of some 35kt, which suggests that its capability against modern, fast CIS Navy submarines is marginal. It has an active/passive head capable of homing attacks, either direct or in programmed search mode.

Type A-184 Torpedo (Italy)

This wire-guided torpedo can be launched from surface ships or submarines against either surface or submarine targets. It has a range of some 8.7 miles (14km) and a speed of some 35kt. The torpedo is controlled from the launching ship until its own acoustic sensors acquire the target, when it is allowed to carry out a normal homing attack. The A-184 is in service with the navies of Italy, Peru and Taiwan.

Above: The A-184 is armed with a high-explosive charge warhead.

Bofors Type 375 Rocket System (Sweden)

Developed in Sweden, this rocket system is in service with at least eight navies. The missile weighs some 55lb (250kg) and carries 220lb (100kg) of TNT or 176lb (80kg) of hexotonal. Fuzes are set automatically at proximity, time or impact. The missile has a rocket motor and follows a flat trajectory, thus minimising time of flight. Maximum range is approximately 2.27 miles (3.65km).

SS-N-14 Silex (CIS)

The tube-launched, rocket-powered SS-N-14 is mounted in most modern CIS surface warships. The missile carries a homing torpedo at a height of 260ft (80m) and a cruising speed of Mach 0.95, under command guidance from the parent ship. The torpedo is released and drops to the water, controlled by a drogue parachute, and then carries out a normal search and homes on the target. It is assumed that, following recent East-West agreements, the nuclear warheads have been withdrawn from service. Range varies from some 5.7 miles (9.17km) in Krivak class frigates to as much as 34.2 miles (55km) in large warships.

SS-N-15/16 (CIS)

The SS-N-15 is carried by most CIS Navy attack submarines. It is an ASW system in which an underwater-launched missile travels to the surface and then follows an airborne flightpath, releasing a nuclear depth bomb near the target. It is believed to be a direct copy of the US SUBROC, which was compromised in 1964. The successor, SS-N-16, carries a homing torpedo with a conventional, as well as a nuclear, warhead.

ASW Rocket Launcher (CIS)

Virtually all CIS surface warships carry at least one ASW rocket launcher, of which there are several varieties. The rockets are fired in a predetermined pattern from a multiple launcher which is remotely trained and elevated. Current models include the RBU 1200 (a five-barrelled 250mm system used in older ships); RBU 2500 (10-barrelled 200mm system, fitted in older cruisers and destroyers and in some small escorts); RBU 6000 (300mm system with twelve barrels arranged in a circular fashion; range about 6,560yd [6,000m]; fitted in many modern warships). A new ten-barrelled large-calibre device (RBU 12000) is fitted in the new carriers.

Stingray (UK)

Stingray can be launched from helicopters, fixed-wing aircraft and surface ships, and is now in service with Egypt, Thailand and the UK. It is an autonomous acoustic-homing torpedo and is claimed to be equally effective in shallow and deep water. An on-board computer can make its own tactical decisions during the course of an attack. Speed is 44kt.

Above: Among the weapons on the foredeck of the CIS Navy battlecruiser *Kirov* are the twin-tube launchers for the SS-N-14 Silex SSM.

Above: A very clear view of an RBU 6000 ASW rocket launcher. There is a great variety of this type of launcher fitted on virtually all CIS warships.

ASROC (USA)

ASROC consists of a Mk 46 torpedo attached to a solid-propellant rocket motor. It is fired either from a box-shaped 8-cell launcher or from the Mk 10 Terrier launcher. On launch, the missile follows a ballistic trajectory and the rocket motor is jettisoned at a predetermined point. The torpedo descends by parachute to the surface, where its homing head and motor are activated. Range is estimated to be 0.31-3.56 miles (0.5-5.7km). This very successful system is in service on some 240 ships of twleve navies. A vertically launched version is also in service. Following East/West agreement nuclear warheads have now been withdrawn.

SUBROC (USA)

SUBROC is a nuclear missile (1KT warhead) designed for use against hostile submarines. It is launched from a standard torpedo tube and after a short underwater journey it rises to the surface and becomes airborne until it returns to the water and the warhead sinks to a set depth before detonating. Range is about 35 miles (56km) and airborne speed in excess of Mach 1; estimated lethal radius of the W-55 warhead is 3-5 miles (5-8km). Most USN SSNs are equipped to carry SUBROC. SUBROC is being withdrawn because of its nuclear warhead and will be replaced by Sea Lance in the mid-1990s.

Above: ASROC missile at the moment of launch from the foredeck of a US frigate. Payload is either a Mk 46 torpedo or a nuclear depth bomb.

Right: Having been launched underwater, SUBROC is now in the air portion of its mission, prior to the torpedo returning to the ocean.

Sea Lance (USA)

Sea Lance (formerly the Anti-Submarine Warfare Stand-Off Weapon, or ASW-SOW) is designed to replace the SUBROC system; it will also be available for launch from surface ships. The missile will be stored in a canister in a standard torpedo tube and on launch the entire canister will leave the submarine and travel to the surface, where the missile motor will ignite, the canister will detach itself and the missile proceed towards the target. The payload will be the new and very effective Mk 50 torpedo; there will not be a nuclear warhead.

Left: An artist's impression of the flight of Boeing's Sea Lance anti-submarine missile. When it eventually comes into service, it will be carried on surface ships as well as in submarines. The warhead is likely to be Mk 50 torpedo, a nuclear warhead will not be carried.

Above: A Boeing ASW-SOW replica test capsule is loaded aboard a submarine for a test firing. This weapon is due to replace the SUBROC.

Above: One of the extremely successful Mk 46 torpedoes installed on an SH-3. This weapon is in use with at least 21 navies.

Mk 46 Torpedo (USA)

This torpedo is used by at least twenty-one navies, and is a deep-diving, high-speed device which can be launched from surface warships, helicopters or fixed-wing aircraft; it can also be carried by the ASROC system. The Mk 46 has an active/passive acoustic homing sensor for its role of submarine attack. The increased speed of CIS SSNs, allied to the Clusterguard paint which seriously attenuates the acoustic response, has given rise to the Near-Term Improvement Program (NEARTIP) which will be both applied to new-production Mk 46s and retrofitted to in-service torpedoes. The Mk 46 is also used in the CAPTOR system, in which an encapsulated torpedo (hence 'CAPTOR') is moored in deep water and then launched on detection of a suitable hostile target. These mines can be delivered by surface ships, aircraft or submarines.

Above: CAPTOR mines loaded on a P-3 Orion. CAPTOR launches its Mk 46 torpedo actively to hunt its target.

MK 50 Torpedo (USA)

The latest CIS submarines are not only faster and capable of diving deeper than previous types, but are also being constructed of new, stronger materials. In addition, they are being coated with anechoic paint or anechoic tiles to reduce the reflective signature. Thus although in-service torpedoes can be improved to a certain extent, the challenge is now such that a totally new torpedo is needed. This programme has led to the Mk 50 torpedo, formerly known as the Advanced Lightweight Torpedo (ALWT). This is the same size and weight as the Mk 46 but is faster and dives deeper. Its speed is reported to be of the order of 60kt, which has been made possible by the unique propulsion system in which the heat of a liquid lithium and sulphur hexafluoride reaction is used to produce steam, which drives the turbine. It can be dropped by aircraft or launched by surface vessels and will enter service in the early 1990s.